1000
ELEGANT PHRASES

1000
ELEGANT PHRASES

By

J. E. Schmidt, M.D., Litt.D.

The Medical Lexicographer of Modern Medicine
Chairman, National Association on Standard
Medical Vocabulary

CHARLES C THOMAS · PUBLISHER
Springfield · Illinois · U.S.A.

Published and Distributed Throughout the World by
CHARLES C THOMAS • PUBLISHER
BANNERSTONE HOUSE
301-327 East Lawrence Avenue, Springfield, Illinois, U.S.A.
NATCHEZ PLANTATION HOUSE
735 North Atlantic Boulevard, Fort Lauderdale, Florida,
U.S.A.

With THOMAS BOOKS careful attention is given to all de-
tails of manufacturing and design. It is the Publisher's desire
to present books that are satisfactory as to their physical
qualities and artistic possibilities and appropriate for their
particular use. THOMAS BOOKS will be true to those laws
of quality that assure a good name and good will.

PE
1670
.S3

Printed in the United States of America
N-1

Introduction

THE ENGLISH LANGUAGE is a multitudinous giant among languages. Its massive vocabulary consists of more than 650,000 words, and it is persistently growing by the acquisition of new terms. The numerousness of the English vocabulary is the result of several factors. The most influential of these are the multinational composition of the American people and the luxurious proliferation of the American arts, sciences, and technologies. Each foreign root of the nation infused into the language a multitude of native terms which in time became assimilated and indistinguishable from the basic Anglo-Saxon.

Among the words of foreign origin that have become completely Americanized we have such workaday and unsophisticated terms as "molasses" (derived from the Portuguese), "slogan" (from Gaelic), "yacht" from the Dutch), "quartz" (from German), "tornado" (from the Spanish), "cameo" (of Italian origin), "tattoo" from Tahitian), "typhoon" (from the Chinese), etc.

Similarly, in the sciences, especially in the biological disciplines, thousands of words have been formed from Greek and Latin roots, to add a potent classic tributary to the voluminous reservoir of the American tongue.

But in spite of its multilingual ancestry and its ample scope, English is still incomplete in itself, even now. Many concepts can be expressed better by a word or phrase borrowed from a foreign language. Some ideas have no

English equivalents at all. It is this need, to fill in certain gaps in the American language, which led to the formation of an important expressional auxiliary consisting of selected words and phrases borrowed from various foreign languages, mainly French, Latin, Italian, and German. These elegant and classic expressions were plucked by the hand of usage, because of their unparalleled excellence in expressing gracefully and pithily certain ideas and concepts for which there are no adequate counterparts in our language. Some of the more familiar ones, as *carte blanche, bon vivant, beau geste, bona fide, en passant,* etc., may already be a part of the reader's vocabulary armamentarium. With many other expressions, however, the reader will probably have only a slight acquaintance, or no acquaintance at all. This book contains a total of 1,000 elegant words, phrases, aphorisms, maxims, epigrams, adages, and mottos.

The semantic quality of the loan-words and loan-phrases through which they express the thought more forcefully, more elegantly, and more succinctly is, therefore, the main reason for their ever increasing popularity. But there are other, ancillary reasons. One is the fact that these exotic expressions have a cultural flavor, an essence, a *je ne sais quoi* which commands attention and respect. Another reason is the fact that the user of these *bons mots,* these delectable literary tidbits, implies with delicacy a background of refinement, an experience of good reading, and an enviable intimacy with the charms of the Classics. Still another motive for using foreign expressions is the characteristic of some of the profounder ones to discharge an emanation of wisdom having a remarkable power of intellectual penetration, as illustrated by the Latin expression *festina lente,* make haste slowly.

The use of foreign grace notes exerts a good influence on the language, which has been deteriorating in the past few decades, especially since the end of World War II. The depreciation has resulted mainly from the introduction into the language of slang terminology and from the careless use of words in general. The recording of the adulterants and the misusage in the revised editions of the standard dictionaries which appeared in recent years tends to abet the faults and to perpetuate the linguistic lesions. (It should be noted, in defense of the dictionary makers, that the recording of abusage is well within the scope of a standard dictionary. It is, in fact, an essential function. Dictionaries are not meant to be judicial, only reportorial.) The use of the elegant foreign expressions acts as an antidote to the undesirable trends, by making the language more attractive and vital, and thus encourages the exercise of greater care in the selection of words and in the use of grammar and rhetoric.

The need for effective communication has never been so keen as it is at present. In these days of increased competition it is not enough for one to have a good idea. One must know how to express it clearly and forcefully—how to "put it across." The use of tired and flabby words is a *passe partout*, a master key, to failure. The classic expressions presented in this book are a potent ingredient for the injection of vigor and elegance into our mechanism of communication.

Thus, *caveat emptor* carries more persuasion than its English translation "let the buyer beware." The French *bon mot* is handsomer, and means more, than the English "apt word." *Con amore* is warmer and more exquisite than its English equivalent "with love." The Gallic *dernier cri* is infinitely more fashionable than the prosaic "latest trend." The Roman *dolus bonus* is a refreshing alternative for "white lie." And *sine qua non* tells more and carries more semantic punch than its English rendition "indispensable thing." The same superior quality resides in *persona non grata, non sequitur, noblesse oblige, joie de vivre, double entendre, donna e mobile, dolce far niente, coup d'etat,* and numerous others.

It is interesting and beneficial to observe that even when a given foreign expression is not expected to be understood by the reader without a translation, it is still advantageous to use it, along with the English translation, for it has been shown by repeated tests that such a citation is psychologically more effective than the English rendition alone.

Formerly, the use of these charming classic expressions —other than the two or three dozen most common ones —was restricted to literary circles. One saw them in the august quarterly journals and in other periodicals catering to the literati. But things have changed. These splendid international words and phrases are seen more and more frequently everywhere, in mass-media magazines (as *Life, Look, Time, Newsweek,* etc.), in newspapers, in novels, in advertising media, on menus, etc., etc. Classic expressions are no longer esoteric literary luxuries. They are expressional status symbols sought and used by many. Everyone who is "somebody"—or who aspires to be a "somebody," or wants at least to make the impression of being a "somebody"—will find this book very useful. The 1,000 entries contained in the book have been carefully selected and meticulously defined, to make them of the utmost value not only to the tyro but also to the savant. The aim of the author has been to make the translations definitive, up-to-date, and, above all, understandable. The expressions and their definitions should be found desirable for their esthetic as well as utilitarian qualities.

As a reference book on the very best in elegant foreign phrases, this volume should be especially attractive and practically useful to authors of both fiction and non-fiction material, to editors (in checking the appropriateness of classic expressions found in submitted manuscripts), to teachers of English and of foreign languages, to students of philology and linguistics, to researchers in the Classics and in history (as well as in anthropology, folklore, and archaeology), to personnel in library reference departments, to ambassadors and diplomats (as well as others in the foreign service), to magazine and newspaper columnists and feature writers, to speakers in the various lecture circuits, to toastmasters and masters of ceremonies, to priests, ministers, and rabbis, to writers of advertising copy, to crossword puzzle fans, to journalists and reporters, to rewrite men, to poets and playwrights, to ghostwriters and "as-told-to-ers," and many others.

Aside from the groups mentioned above, the average reader and the average letter writer will undoubtedly find the *1,000 Elegant Phrases* a gratifying source of literary refreshments. Writers of *billets-doux* will find the book a font of suitable expressions. But this is not all. The man or woman who applies for a job may reflect on the possibility that, everything else being equal, the use of an apt phrase in the letter of application may mean the difference between a polite rejection and a welcome acceptance. Also, the college student and the high school student will find that a selective use of graceful notes in their compositions and theses may result in higher grades.

The *1,000 Elegant Phrases* and their comprehensive definitions form only half of this book. To make the book even more useful, the author prepared an exhaustive index which appears as Part II.

This index, consisting of more than 3,500 entries, is a unique feature which enables the user to find an appropriate Elegant Phrase on the basis of its *meaning.* This is possible because the more than 3,500 entries of the Index are basically the meanings of the Elegant

Phrases, and they are arranged in alphabetical order, with references to Part I of the book.

It is thus possible for the reader who wishes to find an elegant phrase with which to express his own thought to find this thought or idea in the Index, and thus pinpoint the exact elegant phrase which fits the occasion. For instructions on the use of the Index, see *Explanatory Note on the Index*, on page 130.

In conclusion, the author hopes that every user of this book will derive from it a measure of benefit and pleasure, in accordance with his needs.

1000
ELEGANT PHRASES

(1) a ballata (It.)
(Rendered or expressed) in the style of a ballad.

(2) à bas! (F.)
Down with!—an expression of condemnation, protest, disapproval, etc.

(3) à beau jeu beau retour (F.)
For a good deed a good return; blow for blow; retaliation.

(4) à bon dessein (F.)
With a good (or noble) intention.

(5) à bon droit (F.)
With good right; with justice; well deserved.

(6) à bon marché (F.)
At a good bargain; at a good price or rate; cheap.

(7) à bouche ouverte (F.)
With open mouth (in the manner of a young bird); avidly; without discrimination; without critical appraisal.

3

(8)　*à brûle-pourpoint (F.)*

(So close) as to burn the doublet (or jacket) ;—in allusion to shooting at close range; point-blank; to one's
face; in a brusque or rough manner.

(9)　*a capite ad calcem (L.)*

From the head to the heel; from head to foot; all over;
entirely.

(10)　*a cappella (It.)*

In chapel style; without instrumental accompaniment;
—said of choral singing.

(11)　*a capriccio (It.)*

At pleasure (of the performer) ; at the tempo chosen by
the performer; with the expression chosen by the player.

(12)　*à chaque oiseau son nid est beau (F.)*

To each bird its own nest is beautiful; to a mother her
own child is always beautiful; one's own home is most
comfortable and beautiful.

(13)　*à cheval (F.)*

On horseback; with a leg on either side; astride, as
with regard to an issue; on the fence.

(14)　*à coeur ouvert (F.)*

From the open heart; with utmost sincerity; with candor; with honesty and frankness.

(15)　*à compte (F.)*

On account; in part payment; to the credit of an account.

(16)   *à deaux (F.)*

For two; of two; two at a time; for two only; in an intimate manner; private; personal.

(17)   *a die (L.)*

From that day; from then on.

(18)   *a fonte puro pura deuit aqua (L.)*

From a pure fountain, pure flows the water; from a clean mind come clean thoughts; from a noble family come noble offspring.

(19)   *à genoux (F.)*

On (one's) knees; in a kneeling posture; humbly.

(20)   *à grands frais (F.)*

At great expense; at considerable sacrifice.

(21)   *à haute voix (F.)*

In high voice; in loud tones; aloud.

(22)   *à la fin (F.)*

In the end; at the end; at last; at long last; finally.

(23)   *à la grecque (F.)*

In the Greek fashion; in the Greek style; as the Greeks do it.

(24)   *à la lettre (F.)*

To the letter; *literatim;* literally; precisely.

(25)   *à la mort (F.)*

1. To the death; fatally; at the point of death.
2. Melancholy; depressed.

(26)   *à la volee (F.)*

On the fly or wing; in the air; without thinking; hastily; seizing the occasion.

(27)   *a minori ad majus (L.)*

From the less to the greater; from the less important to the more important;—said of the factors in an argument, of evidence, etc.

(28)   *a natura rei (L.)*

From the nature of the thing; from the nature of the case; by the very nature of the situation.

(29)   *a novo (L.)*

Anew; from the beginning; all over again.

(30)   *a poco a poco (It.)*

Little by little; gradually.

(31)   *à point (F.)*

To the point; to the exact point; just in time; at the opportune time; to a nicety; just so; just right.

(32)   *a posteriori (L.)*

From what comes later; from what follows; from the latter; from effect to cause; based on experience; from the particular to the general.

(33)   *a prima vista (It.)*

At first sight; at first glance; from the very beginning.

(34)   *a priori (L.)*

From what comes first; from cause to effect; from a generalization to a particular case; based on theory rather than experience. Opposed to *a posteriori.*

(35) *à quoi bon? (F.)*

For what good? For what purpose? Of what use (is it)? What is to be gained from it?

(36) *à rebours (F.)*

The wrong way; against the grain; against the fur; backward.

(37) *a teneris annis (L.)*

From the tender years; from the early years; from childhood.

(38) *a tergo (L.)*

From behind; from the back; from the rear.

(39) *à tort (F.)*

The wrong way; wrongly; wrong.

(40) *à tort et à droit (F.)*

(Both) wrong and right; regardless of wrong and right; rightly or wrongly.

(41) *à tort et à travers (F.)*

Wrong and awry; at cross purposes; at random; without discrimination; regardless of outcome.

(42) *à tout hasard (F.)*

At any risk; at any price; at any hazard.

(43) *à tout prix (F.)*

At all cost; at any price.

(44) *a verbis ad verbera (L.)*

From words to punches; from an argument to fisticuffs.

(45)　*à vieux comptes nouvelles disputes (F.)*

New disputes on old accounts; new arguments on old subjects.

(46)　*a viva voce (It.)*

With a living voice; by word of mouth; orally, rather than by the printed word.

(47)　*ab absurdo (L.)*

From absurdity; said of an argument or reason which is rejected because of its alleged inconsistency with what is regarded as reasonable.

(48)　*ab aeterno (L.)*

From eternity (till the present time) ; always; from time immemorial.

(49)　*ab agendo (L.)*

(Put) out of action, as by illness; disabled; unfit; incapacitated; disqualified; ineligible.

(50)　*ab antiquo (L.)*

From antiquity; from days of old; of yore.

(51)　*ab igne ignem (L.)*

From fire (comes) fire; from dangerous means come equally dangerous consequences; radical methods invite radical reactions.

(52)　*ab incunabulis (L.)*

From the cradle; from one's infancy or childhood; from one's earliest recollections.

(53)　*ab integro (L.)*

From a fresh beginning; anew; from a new start.

(54) ab origine (L.)

From the origin (of the thing) ; from the beginning.

(55) ab uno disce omnes (L.)

All learn from one; many learn from one (good example) ; everybody learns from somebody.

(56) Aberglaube (G.)

Superstition; belief in the supernatural; belief in omens, charms, etc.

(57) absit invidia (L.)

Let there be no ill will; let there be no jealousy or envy; let there be no hatred; let there be no offense.

(58) absit verbo invidia (L.)

May there be no ill will in the saying; may there be no offense in the words;—a prefatory remark about a statement which may sound boastful, disparaging, etc.

(59) absolvi meam animam (L.)

I have unburdened my mind; I have gotten it off my chest;—said with regard to the relief gained through a confession, the performance of an act of duty, etc.

(60) abundans cautela non nocet (L.)

An abundance of caution does not hurt; excessive caution does no harm; one cannot be too careful.

(61) abundant dulcibus vitiis (L.)

They abound with charming faults; they have many delightful moral failings; they do not lack in agreeable debauchery.

(62) *abusus non tollit usum (L.)*

Abuse does not contraindicate use; i.e., the misuse of something is not a reason against proper usage.

(63) *actum ne agas (L.)*

Do not do that which is already done.

(64) *acu rem tetigisti (L.)*

You have touched the matter with a needle; you have pinpointed the thing; you hit the nail on the head.

(65) *ad bivium (L.)*

At the crossroads; at the junction of two roads.

(66) *ad captandum (L.)*

For the purpose of appealing (or captivating) ;—said of a maneuver, argument, plea, etc., intended to have its effect on prejudices, passions, sentiments, desires, etc., rather than reason.

(67) *ad cautelam (L.)*

As a precautionary measure; as a preventive; as a safeguard.

(68) *ad eundem (L.)*

To the same (rank or degree) ;—said especially with regard to the transfer of a student from one university to another, on the same level, without examination.

(69) *ad extremum virium (L.)*

To the extreme of one's strength; to the utmost of one's ability.

(70) ad finem (L.)

To the (very) end; at the end.

(71) ad gloriam (L.)

For glory; without remuneration; without pay; not for money.

(72) ad hoc (L.)

For this; for this case only; pertaining only to this; —said especially with regard to an argument which applies to a specific case, but not to others.

(73) ad honorem (L.)

For honor; for an honorary purpose; for the honor to be derived, as from an act.

(74) ad idem (L.)

At the same; to the same end or effect; in agreement; —said of proposals offered in the formulation of a contract.

(75) ad infinitum (L.)

To infinity; without limit; endlessly.

(76) ad initium (L.)

To the beginning; at the beginning.

(77) ad interim (L.)

In the meantime; meanwhile; temporary.

(78) ad judicium (L.)

To the judgment (of the mind); to common sense. See also under *argumentum ad judicium.*

(79)   *ad lib. (L.)*

A short form of *ad libitum*, which see.

(80)   *ad libitum (L.)*

At pleasure; in the manner that one wishes; as much as one wishes; as often as one wishes. Also written *ad lib.*

(81)   *ad litteram (L.)*

To the letter; exactly; literally;—said of a quotation, translation, etc.

(82)   *ad longum (L.)*

At length; in a prolix manner.

(83)   *ad meliora vertamur (L.)*

Let us turn to better things; let us turn to pleasanter subjects; let us speak of happier things; let us change the subject.

(84)   *ad multos annos! (L.)*

For many years! To a long life! To a long rule!

(85)   *ad nauseam (L.)*

To (the point of) nausea; to the point of disgust; to a disgusting extreme; revoltingly excessive.

(86)   *ad unum (L.)*

To (the last) one; to the last man; everybody; all; unanimously.

(87)   *ad valorem (L.)*

According to the value (involved); in proportion to the value;—said especially in reference to duties on goods. Also written *ad val.*

(88) ad vitam aeternam (L.)
For life eternal; for eternity; forever.

(89) Adeste fideles (L.)
Be present ye faithful;—a Latin Christmas hymn.

(90) advocatus diaboli (L.)
A devil's advocate;—i.e., a person who defends the side, in an argument, which is regarded as wrong, often merely to bring out the facts; a destructive critic; one who perversely upholds a base cause.

(91) aegrescitque medendo (L.)
And he grows worse with treatment; and it worsens when treated; the treatment is worse than the disease; hence, leave well enough alone.

(92) aegri somnia (L.)
The dreams of a sick man. See also *aegri somnia vana.*

(93) aegri somnia vana (L.)
The vain dreams of a sick man; empty dreams; impossible dreams.

(94) aequam memento rebus in arduis servare mentem (L.)
Remember to preserve a calm mind in difficult circumstances; keep your shirt on. Also shortened to *aequam servare mentem.*

(95) aequanimiter (L.)
With equanimity; with calmness of mind; with evenness of temper.

(96) aequo animo (L.)

With evenness of mind; with equanimity; with calmness; with serenity; with composure.

(97) Agnus Dei (L.)

Lamb of God; a pictorial representation of Christ as a lamb; a small wax disk bearing the picture of a lamb.

(98) aide-mémoire (F.)

Memory aid; mnemonic device; something to aid the memory, as a summary of a proceeding, agreement, etc.; a memorandum.

(99) alea jacta est (L.)

The die is cast; it's all decided; the fate is sealed.

(100) alienatus a se (L.)

Alienated from himself; not in one's right mind; insane.

(101) alieni temporis flores (L.)

The flowers of a bygone time; the prime of other days; the glory of yesteryear.

(102) alternis vicibus (L.)

Alternately; taking alternate turns; in shifts.

(103) altum silentium (L.)

High silence; profound or deep silence.

(104) amabilis insania (L.)

An agreeable form of madness; a pleasing insanity; a delightful peculiarity.

(105) *amare et sapere vix deo conceditur (L.)*

To love and to be wise (at the same time) is scarcely granted even to a god; one who is in love can scarcely be expected to be wise or to exercise good judgment; love is blind.

(106) *amari aliquid (L.)*

Something bitter; something unpleasant.

(107) *âme damnée (F.)*

A damned soul; a minion; a willing and blind tool of another's will; one who is devoted and slavishly obedient to another.

(108) *âme de boue (F.)*

A soul made of mud; a depraved person; an evil-minded person; a person having base tendencies.

(109) *âme perdue (F.)*

A lost soul; a person morally debased; a person mired in depravity.

(110) *amende honorable (F.)*

Honorable reparation or amends; a formal and humble apology to an offended person; a full acknowledgment of one's error accompanied by a humiliating apology.

(111) *amicus curiae (L.)*

A friend of the court;—a person, often a layman, who advises the court in some special field in which he is well informed.

(112) *amor nummi (L.)*

Love of money; greediness, cupidity.

(113)   amour-propre (F.)

1. Self-love; self-esteem; self-respect. 2. Excessive self-esteem; vanity.

(114)   ancipitis usus (L.)

Having a two-headed (twofold) application or use; having a dobule advantage; having a twofold benefit.

(115)   ancora imparo (It.)

I am still learning;—a saying attributed to Michelangelo.

(116)   anguis in herba (L.)

A snake in the grass; an unsuspected danger; an enemy pretending to be a friend.

(117)   aniles fabulae (L.)

Old wives' tales; tales told by old women; unlikely stories.

(118)   animo et corpore (L.)

With (both) mind and body; with both thought and act; with intention backed by action.

(119)   animo et facto (L.)

In intention and in fact; in intention and in action. See also *animo et corpore.*

(120)   animo et fide (L.)

With courage and faith.

(121)   animo, non astutia (L.)

By means of courage, not by craft.

(122)   anno ante Christum (L.)
In the year before Christ, i.e., B.C.

(123)   anno Christi (L.)
In the year of Christ, i.e., A.D.

(124)   anno Domini (L.)
In the year of the Lord, i.e., A.D.

(125)   anno hebraico (L.)
In the Hebrew year; of the Hebrew calendar.

(126)   anno mundi (L.)
In the year of the world; i.e., reckoning from the time of the supposed creation of the world, in 4004 B.C.

(127)   ante Christum (L.)
Before (the birth of) Christ;—used in reckoning time; A.C.; B.C.

(128)   ante litem motam (L.)
Before the litigation began; before the argument began; before the controversy began.

(129)   ante meridiem (L.)
Before midday; before noon; A.M.

(130)   antipasto (It.)
An appetizer served before a meal; something that whets the appetite.

(131)   apage Satanas! (L.)
Get thee hence, Satan! Go away, Devil!

(132) *apparatus criticus (L.)*
Critical apparatus; reference books, texts, etc., used by authors in literary work.

(133) *après coup (F.)*
After the stroke; too late to do good.

(134) *après la mort, le médicin (F.)*
After death (of the patient), the doctor; too late.

(135) *aquila non capit muscas (L.)*
An eagle does not catch flies; a great man does not occupy himself with trifles; a champion does not work for peanuts.

(136) *arbiter elegantiarum (L.)*
A judge of elegance; a judge of good taste; a person fastidious in his tastes; an exquisite.

(137) *arbiter morum (L.)*
A judge of morals; an authority on the subject of conduct.

(138) *arcanum arcanorum (L.)*
The mystery of mysteries; the ultimate secret.

(139) *ardentia verba (L.)*
Ardent words; burning words; heated words; glowing language.

(140) *arena sine calce (L.)*
Sand without lime; words without substance; arguments that do not support each other.

(141) *argumentum ad judicium (L.)*

An argument addressed to a person's good sense, reasoning, judgment, etc.

(142) *argumentum ad misercordiam (L.)*

An argument intended to appeal to the listener's feelings, sympathy, pity, etc.

(143) *argumentum ex concesso (L.)*

An argument based on what has already been conceded.

(144) *ariston metron (Gr.)*

Moderation (is) best; middle-of-the-road course is best; moderate measures are best.

(145) *artium baccalaureus (L.)*

Bachelor of arts; A.B.; B.A.

(146) *artium magister (L.)*

Master of arts; M.A.

(147) *at spes non fracta (L.)*

And yet hope is not weakened (or crushed); there is still hope.

(148) *au fait (F.)*

To the fact; acquainted with the matter at hand; having knowledge of the thing; well versed; expert; proficient.

(149) *au naturel (F.)*

In the natural state; naked; true to life; as it occurs in nature; simple; simply; unadorned.

(150) au revoir (F.)

To see again; until we see each other again; till we meet again; good-by for now; *auf Wiedersehen.*

(151) auctor ignotus (L.)

An unknown author; an author who is not widely known; an author whose work is not fully appreciated.

(152) aude sapere (L.)

Dare to be wise; dare to do the right thing.

(153) audi alteram partem (L.)

Hear the other side (in a controversy, before passing judgment).

(154) audiatur et altera pars (L.)

Give the other side (in a controversy) a chance to be heard.

(155) audio sed taceo (L.)

I hear but I remain silent; I listen but I do not judge.

(156) auf Wiedersehen (G.)

To see again; till we meet again; good-by for now; *au revoir.*

(157) aurea mediocritas (L.)

The golden mean; the happy middle of the road; the happy medium.

(158) aut non tentaris perfice (L.)

Either do not try, or complete; either do not start, or else finish.

(159) *aux grands maux, les grands remèdes (F.)*

For critical diseases, desperate remedies; difficult problems require radical solutions; unusual situations call for unusual measures.

(160) *avec entrain (F.)*

With spirit; with animation; ardently; warmly; heartily.

(161) *avise la fin (F.)*

Perceive the end; consider the outcome.

(162) *ayant droit (F.)*

In law, a party to whom the rights of another have been transferred.

(163) baptême du feu (F.)

A baptism of fire; an arduous ordeal; the fiirst exposure to extreme danger, as in battle; a soldier's first experience under enemy fire.

(164) bar mitzvah (Heb.)

A man of duty or responsibility. In Hebrew religion, a boy who has reached his thirteenth year and has thus become responsible for the observance of the religious law; also, the ceremony marking the assumption of this responsibility.

(165) beatae memoriae (L.)

Of blessed memory; of beatified memory; having happy associations.

(166) beau désordre (F.)

Beautiful disorder; pleasing confusion; disorderly life; licentiousness.

(167) beau geste (F.)

A beautiful gesture; a noble act; a fine act. Also, an act or a gesture which seems noble or fine but is devoid of substance; an empty gesture.

(168) beau monde (F.)

The beautiful world; the elegant world; the world of fashion; fashionable society; high society.

(169) beauté du diable (F.)

The beauty of the devil; the bloom of youth; beauty which bewitches; tormenting attractiveness.

(170) beaux-arts (F.)

The beautiful arts; the fine arts; the graphic arts.

(171) bel air (F.)

Fine air; fine bearing; cultured deportment; the air of high society.

(172) bel canto (It.)

Beautiful song; a style of singing marked by skillful vocal display; singing characterized by virtuosity and purity of tone.

(173) bel esprit (pl. beaux esprits) (F.)

Beautiful spirit; a clever person; a brilliant mind; a highly intellectual person; a wit.

(174) bella, horrida bella! (L.)

Wars, horrible wars!

(175) belle assemblée (F.)

A fashionable gathering; an assembly of stylish persons.

(176) belle narras (L.)

You say it well; you tell it splendidly.

(177) belle vue (F.)

A fine view; a fair outlook; a beautiful prospect.

(178) belles-lettres (F.)

Beautiful letters; fine literature; literature as a form of art; literature having aesthetic value.

(179) bellum omnium in omnes (L.)

A war of all against all; a war of each against all.

(180) ben trovato (It.)

Well found; well conceived; well invented; well expressed; well done.

(181) bene decessit (L.)

He departed well; he left under favorable conditions.

(182) bene merentibus (L.)

To the well-deserving; to those who merit.

(183) bene nati, bene vestiti, et mediocriter docti (L.)

(He is) well born, well dressed, and (only) moderately well learned.

(184) bene vale! (L.)

Farewell! Good-by! Take good care!

(185) bene vobis! (L.)

All good with you! Health to you! To your health!

(186) beneficium invito non datur (L.)

A benefit cannot be bestowed on one who is unwilling.

(187)   beneplacito (L.)

At your pleasure; during your pleasure; by your permission.

(188)   benigno numine (L.)

With a favoring god; with a kindly fate; with good luck.

(189)   besser Rat kommt über Nacht (G.)

Better advice comes after the night; better counsel comes in the morning, after a night's sleep; one sees things clearer after "sleeping" on them for a while.

(190)   bien-aimé (fem. bien-aimée) (F.)

Well beloved; dear; cherished one; sweetheart.

(191)   bien-être (F.)

Well-being; comfort; restfulness; soundness of body; robustness; euphoria.

(192)   bien fondé (F.)

Well established; well founded; well grounded; demonstrated; secure; stable; settled.

(193)   bien-pensant (F.)

Right-thinking; well-disposed; orthodox.

(194)   bienséance (F.)

Something which is proper; that which is fittting; decency; decorum; seemliness.

(195)   bienvenue (F.)

A celebration marking the admission of a person to the membership of a society; the admission to a society or association.

(196)   billet d'amour (F.)

A love note; a love letter.

(197)   billet-doux (pl. billets doux) (F.)

Same as *billet d'amour*, which see.

(198)   bis dat quit cito dat (L.)

He gives twice who gives forthwith; help given promptly is twice appreciated.

(199)   bis pueri senes (L.)

Old men (are) boys twice; old men are twice childish.

(200)   bon jour (F.)

Good day; good morning; hello.

(201)   bon soir (F.)

Good evening;—a salutation.

(202)   bon vivant (F.)

A person who loves good living; a person devoted to good food and the pleasures of life; a gourmet.

(203)   bon viveur (F.)

One who is dedicated to a life of pleasure; one who lives a fast life; a person devoted to good living.

(204)   bon voyage! (F.)

A good voyage; Pleasant journey!—a wish expressed to one who is leaving.

(205)   bona fide (L.)

In good faith; with sincerity; genuinely; without intention to deceive.

(206) bona si sua norint (L.)

It would be good if they appreciated their blessings; if only they were aware of their blessings.

(207) bonne nuit (F.)

Good night; a good night; a pleasant night; a night of pleasure.

(208) bonnet de nuit (F.)

A nightcap; an alcoholic drink taken before retiring for the night.

(209) bonus vir semper tiro (L.)

A good man is one who always learns.

(210) bouffant (fem. bouffante) (F.)

Puffed; bulging; protuberant; billowy.

(211) bourgeoisie (F.)

1. The middle class of society; those between the very wealthy and the working class. 2. The rich people or capitalists, as opposed to the working class.

(212) bravissimo! (It.)

Excellent! Splendid! Extremely well done!

(213) *cacoëthes carpendi (L.)*

An uncontrollable urge to criticize and find fault with the actions, opinions, etc., of others.

(214) *cacoëthes loquendi (L.)*

An uncontrollable desire to speak or make orations.

(215) *cacoëthes scribendi (L.)*

An uncontrollable desire to write or to be an author.

(216) *cadit quaestio (L.)*

The question falls down; the argument collapses; the case under consideration is closed.

(217) *caeca invidia est (L.)*

Envy is blind; envy deprives one of the ability to think clearly and without bias.

(218) *caelitus mihi vires (L.)*

My strength comes from heaven.

(219) *café au lait (F.)*

Coffee with milk; the color of coffee with milk, i.e., light brown.

(220)   café noir (F.)

Black coffee; the color of coffee without milk, i.e., black.

(221)   cantatrice (pl. cantatrici) (It.)
A female professional singer.

(222)   capriccio (It.)

A whim; a caprice; a prank; a lively or whimsical musical composition.

(223)   carte blanche (pl. cartes blanches) (F.)

A white card; a blank card; a paper bearing only the giver's signature, allowing the bearer to fill in any conditions desired; freedom to do as one pleases; full authority.

(224)   casus necessitatis (L.)

A case of (sheer) necessity.

(225)   causa honoris (L.)

For the sake of honor; for the sake of honoring, as in conferring an honorary degree.

(226)   Cena Domini (L.)
The Lord's Supper.

(227)   censor librorum (L.)
A book censor; a book critic.

(228)   certum voto pete finem (L.)

Look for a definite limit in your desire; set a limit to your ambitions or yearnings.

(229)   *c'est entendu (F.)*

It is understood; it is accepted; it is agreed.

(230)   *c'est la guerre (F.)*

It is war; such is (the nature or hadship of) war; such are the hazards of war; it cannot be helped, because this is wartime.

(231)   *c'est magnifique (F.)*

It is magnificent; it is splendid.

(232)   *cetera quis nescit? (L.)*

Who does not know the rest? Everyone knows the rest.

(233)   *chanson (F.)*

1. A song; a ballad. 2. Poem; poetry; epic. 3. Humbug; stuff; trash; pointless story.

(234)   *chansonnette (F.)*

A short song; a little song; a ditty; a comic song.

(235)   *chanteuse (F.)*

A female singer; a girl singer with a band.

(236)   *chaparajos (Mex. Sp.)*

A kind of leather trousers worn by cowboys over the regular trousers, as a protection for the legs.

(237)   *che sarà sarà (It.)*

What will be, will be; what must come, will come.

(238)   *chef de cuisine (F.)*

The head cook, as in a hotel, restaurant, etc.

(239)   chef-d'oeuvre (pl. chefs-d'oeuvre) (F.)

The principal work, as of an author; a masterpiece, esp. in art, literature, etc.

(240)   cher ami (fem. chère amie) (F.)

Dear friend; beloved friend; cherished friend.

(241)   cherchez la femme (F.)

Look for the woman (in the case);—a facetious implication that a woman is invariably the cause of the trouble.

(242)   chéri (fem. chérie) (F.)

Beloved; dear; darling; cherished one; sweetheart.

(243)   chez (F.)

At the house of; in the home of; among; with; in the service of.

(244)   Christo et ecclesiae (L.)

For Christ and the church.

(245)   cineri gloria sera venit (L.)

Glory comes late when it comes to one's ashes, i.e., after one's death.

(246)   circa (L.)

About (the time or year stated);—used in connection with a date about which the author is uncertain.

(247)   circum (L.)

Around; surrounding; about.

(248) clair de lune (F.)

The light of the moon; moonlight; a pale-blue glaze, as of porcelain.

(249) classes aisées (F.)

The classes of society in easy circumstances; the rich; the well-to-do classes.

(250) clavam extorquere Herculi (L.)

To wring or wrest the club from Hercules; to attempt something extremely hazardous; to try the impossible.

(251) coeur de lion (F.)

The heart of a lion; a man of courage; a brave man.

(252) cogito, ergo sum (L.)

I think, therefore I am; I think, therefore I exist;—a postulate of the philosopher Descartes.

(253) cognatio movit invidiam (L.)

Kinship kindles ill will; familiarity breeds contempt.

(254) cognoscente (pl. cognoscenti) (It.)

A connoisseur; an expert, as in art; a critical judge.

(255) coiffeur (F.)

A hairdresser; a person who dresses women's hair.

(256) compos mentis (L.)

Sane in mind; of sound mind; of sound mind and understanding.

(257) con amore (It.)

With love; with tenderness; with emotion; with zest.

(258)   con brio (It.)
With spirit; with zest.

(259)   con diligenza (It.)
With diligence; with care; with perseverance.

(260)   conjunctis viribus (L.)
With united powers.

(261)   constantia et virtute (L.)
By perseverance and virtue; by constancy and virtue.

(262)   consummatum est (L.)
It is finished; it is completed; it is done.

(263)   contra bonos mores (L.)
Against good mores or manners; against accepted
methods; against morals.

*(264)   contra malum mortis non est medicamen
             in hortis (L.)*
Against the evil of death there is no medicine in the
garden.

(265)   contra mundum (L.)
Against the world;—said of one who defies universal
opinion.

(266)   copia verborum (L.)
Plenty of words; an abundance of words.

(267)   coram paribus (L.)
Before one's equals; before one's peers.

(268)   cordon bleu (F.)

Blue ribbon; the blue ribbon once worn by Knights of the Order of the Holy Ghost; a person entitled to wear the blue ribbon; high distinction; a person of high distinction.

(269)   corpus delicti (L.)

The body of the crime or offense; the facts proving the crime or offense; the substantial facts which constitute the crime charged; incorrectly, but popularly, the body of the victim in a case of murder.

(270)   corpus juris (L.)

A body of law; a collection of all the laws, as of a given country.

(271)   Corpus Juris Canonici (L.)

The canons of the Roman Catholic Church issued up to 1918.

(272)   corrigenda (L.) pl.

A list of errors with their corrections, as in a book.

(273)   coup (F.)

A blow; a stroke; a sudden and successful move; a clever act; a brilliant maneuver.

(274)   coup de grâce (F.)

A stroke of mercy; a shot or blow which brings death to, and ends the suffering of, a victim; any death blow; a stroke which brings something to an end.

(275)   coup d'état (F.)

A stroke of state; a sudden and forceful political move; a sudden overthrow of the established government; a revolutionary stroke.

(276)   courage sans peur (F.)

Courage without fear; daring without apprehension.

(277)   crème de la crème (F.)

Cream of the cream; the best of the best; the very best.

(278)   crève-coeur (F.)

Heartbreak; great sorrow; overwhelming grief; grave disappointment.

(279)   crime passionnel (F.)

A crime of passion; a crime motivated by love, esp. unrequited love; a crime impelled by sexual desire.

(280)   crimen falsi (L.)

The crime of falsifying; forgery; deceit.

(281)   crimen quos inquinat, aequat (L.)

Crime makes equals of those it corrupts.

(282)   croix de guerre (F.)

A French military award or decoration honoring bravery in action.

(283)   cruda viridisque senectus (L.)

A vigorous and green (youthful) old age.

(284) crux interpretum (L.)

A puzzle for translators; a puzzle for interpreters.

(285) crux medicorum (L.)

A puzzling thing for physicians.

(286) cucullus non facit monachum (L.)

A hood does not make the monk; clothes do not make the man.

(287) cui bono? (L.)

For whose good? For whose benefit? For what purpose?

(288) cuique suum (L.)

To each one his own (kind).

(289) culpa levis (L.)

A minor fault; a light transgression.

(290) culpae poena par esto (L.)

Let the punishment be commensurate with the crime.

(291) cum bona venia (L.)

With your kind pardon; with your kind indulgence; with your kind permission.

(292) cum grano salis (L.)

With a grain of salt; with a certain amount of skepticism; with some allowance for exaggeration.

(293) cum laude (L.)

With praise (for excellent accomplishment) ;—said esp. of a graduate from a college, or of the graduation, to signify high standing.

(294)   *cum multis aliis (L.)*

With many others; with many other things.

(295)   *cum notis variorum (L.)*

With notes of various (scholars) ; with notes by many commentators;—said esp. of a literary work.

(296)   *cum permissu superiorum (L.)*

With the permission of the superiors; with the permission of those in charge.

(297) Dämmerschlaf (G.)

Twilight sleep; partial sleep; a condition of partial anesthesia.

(298) damnant quod non intelligunt (L.)

They condemn that which they do not understand.

(299) damnosa hereditas (L.)

A harmful inheritance; an unpleasant legacy.

(300) danse macabre (F.)

The dance of death; a dancing procession in which a skeleton, representing death, leads other skeletons to their grave.

(301) danseur (F.)

A male dancer, esp. a professional dancer; a male professional ballet dancer.

(302) danseuse (F.)

A professional female dancer, esp. a ballet dancer.

(303) dare fatis vela (L.)

To give the sails to destiny (or fate); to sail where the winds blow; to let fate decide; to let things go as they may; to leave decisions in the hands of destiny.

(304) de aequitate (L.)

By equity; by justice; in fairness.

(305) de fumo in flammam (L.)

From the smoke into the flame; from bad to worse; from the frying pan into the fire; from one bad situation into another equally bad or worse.

(306) de gratia (L.)

By grace; by favor.

(307) de profundis (L.)

Out of the depths; out of the depths of misery; out of the depths of feeling.

(308) de propaganda fide (L.)

For the propagation of the faith.

(309) de règle (F.)

According to regular procedure; according to normal form; according to the rule.

(310) de te fabula narratur (L.)

Of you the story is told; change the name, and the story fits you.

(311) debellare superbos (L.)

To subdue the haughty; to conquer the proud; to vanquish those who consider themselves superior.

(312) debemur morti, nos nostraque (L.)

We are bound to death, we and ours; we are mortal, we and our works.

(313)   *debito justitiae (L.)*

By the debt of justice; as a debt to justice.

(314)   *debitum naturae (L.)*

The debt (one owes) to nature; one's life; death.

(315)   *débouché (F.)*

An exit; an outlet, as for emotions.

(316)   *décolletage (F.)*

A low neckline of a dress, esp. one that bares the swell of the breasts and part of the line of cleavage between them.

(317)   *Dei gratia (L.)*

By the grace of God.

(318)   *Dei judicium (L.)*

The judgment of God; trial by ordeal.

(319)   *démarche (F.)*

A policy of action; a change of policy; a new line of action.

(320)   *Deo adjuvante (L.)*

With God's help; God helping; God willing.

(321)   *Deo gratias (L.)*

Thanks to God; with God's kindness.

(322)   *desiderium (L.)*

An ardent wish; a passionate desire; an intense longing; a feeling of loss; sorrow for something unattained or lost; grief.

(323) desipere in loco (L.)

To act foolishly (playfully) at times (or in the right place); to trifle at the proper time; to let down one's hair now and then.

(324) Deus misereatur nostri (L.)

God be merciful unto us; God have compassion for us.

(325) Deus vobiscum (L.)

God be with you.

(326) dicamus bona verba (L.)

Let us speak good words; let us speak auspicious words; let us speak words having a good omen.

(327) dignus vindice nodus (L.)

A difficulty worthy of its resolver; a knotty situation worthy of any expert; a most intricate problem.

(328) dimidium facti, qui coepit, habet (L.)

He has half done who has begun.

(329) divide et impera (L.)

Divide and rule; cause discord among your subjects in order to keep control.

(330) docendo discimus (L.)

By teaching we (also) learn.

(331) doctus cum libro (L.)

Learned with a book; learned with book knowledge; having book learning.

(332) dolce (It.)

Sweet; sweet and soft; soft and smooth, applied esp. to music.

(333) doloroso (It.)

With a plaintive characeristic; in a sorrowful mood.

(334) domat omnia virtus (L.)

Virtue conquers all; virtue overcomes all temptations.

(335) Domine, dirige nos (L.)

Lord, direct us; Lord, show us the way.

(336) Dominus illuminatio mea (L.)

The Lord (is) my enlightenment;—the motto of Oxford University.

(337) Dominus vobiscum (L.)

The Lord (be) with you.

(338) donec corrigatur (L.)

Until (such time as) it shall be corrected.

(339) donna è mobile (It.)

Woman is changeable (in mind); woman is changeable in affection; woman is fickle.

(340) douceur (F.)

Sweetness; fragrance; kindness; a tip; a gratuity; a gift; a bribe.

(341) doyen (fem. doyenne) (F.)

The senior member, as of a professional group; a dean; an elder.

(342)   droit d'asile (F.)

The right of asylum; the right of sanctuary.

(343)   Droit du Seigneur (F.)

An old religious custom which demanded sexual abstinence on the wedding night as "God's right."

(344)   droit et loyal (F.)

Righteous and loyal; sincere and fair.

(345)   ducit amor patriae (L.)

The love of (one's) country guides; patriotism serves
as a guide.

(346)   ducunt volentem fata, nolentem trahunt (L.)

The fates guide the willing (man), the unwilling they
drag along.

(347)   dum fervet opus (L)

While the work is hot; while the inspiration of the
work prevails; while one is in the mood; while in the
heat of action; while the iron is hot.

(348)   dum tacent, clamant (L.)

While they are silent, they are full of voice (they cry
out); their silence is eloquent.

(349)   dum vita est, spes est (L.)

While there is life, there is hope.

(350)   e consensu gentium (L.)

From the consensus of opinion of all people; from the universally held opinion.

(351)   e multis paleis paulum fructus collegi (L.)

From much chaff I have gathered a little bit of grain; I have obtained a small benefit from a great deal of effort.

(352)   e pluribus unum (L.)

One out of many;—the motto of the United States.

(353)   ébauche (F.)

An incompleted work of art; a first, roughhewn form of a sculpture; a rough sketch; an outline, as of a plot; a draft.

(354)   ecce homo! (L.)

Behold the man! Behold Christ!—words said to have been used by Pilate in presenting Christ under the crown of thorns.

(355)   éclat (F.)

A burst; an explosion; a display of brilliance; splendor; acclaim; applause; a demonstration of approval.

(356) école de droit (F.)
A law school.

(357) école de médecine (F.)
A school of medicine.

(358) école des beaux-arts (F.)
A school teaching the fine arts.

(359) écrasons l'infâme (F.)
Let us crush the sordid thing;—an expression attributed to Voltaire with regard to intolerance, superstition, etc.

(360) éditeur (F.)
An editor; a redactor; a publisher.

(361) editio princeps (L.)
The first edition, as of a book; a copy of a first edition.

(362) eheu, fugaces labuntur anni (L.)
Alas, the fleeting years glide by.

(363) ejusdem generis (L.)
Of the same origin; of the same descent; of the same birth; of the same stock; of the same race.

(364) élan (F.)
Ardor; dash; vigor; bound; eagerness for action; burst of enthusiasm.

(365) elixir vitae (L.)
The elixir of life; a hypothetical medicine, sought by alchemists, to confer immortality.

(366) empire des lettres (F.)

The empire of letters; the domain of literature; the realm of learning; the work or profession of an author.

(367) en ami (F.)

As a friend; like a friend.

(368) en avant (F.)

Into the future; onward; forward; march on.

(369) en masse (F.)

In a mass; in a body; in a group; as one unit; all together; altogether; as a whole.

(370) en mauvaise odeur (F.)

In bad odor; in bad favor; in ill repute; in bad taste.

(371) en passant (F.)

In passing; incidentally; by the way; in the course of an event or a procedure; without emphasis; coolly; in an offhand manner.

(372) en pure perte (F.)

In pure waste; in complete loss; in vain; futilely; without gain; without result.

(373) en rapport (F.)

In sympathetic relationship; in close relationship; in accord; in harmony; in agreement.

(374) en résumé (F.)

In recapitulation; in summary; on the whole; to sum up.

(375) en tout (F.)

In all; all together; counting all.

(376) en vérité (F.)

In truth; in all honesty; to be frank; verily; in fact; really.

(377) ennuyé (F.)

Affected with ennui; overcome with weariness and dissatisfaction; tired and bored because of inactivity; wearied by lack of interest in anything.

(378) entre deux feux (F.)

Between two fires; under two assaults; under attack from both sides; faced with two equally harassing situations.

(379) entre nous (F.)

Between us; between ourselves; confidentially.

(380) entrepreneur (fem. entrepreneuse) (F.)

A person who undertakes a business, esp. an offbeat enterprise, involving considerable risk, for the sake of profit and adventure; an adventurous businessman.

(381) entrez (F.)

Come in; enter;—used as an invitation or an imperative.

(382) ergo (L.)

Therefore; hence; for this reason; consequently.

(383) errare est humanum (L.)

To err is human.

(384)   erst wägen, dann wagen (G.)

First (one ought to) weigh, then dare; first consider, then dare; think before you leap.

(385)   esprit (F.)

Spirit; vivacity; lively wit; sprightly cleverness; sparkling intelligence; delicate and bright humor.

(386)   esprit de corps (F.)

The spirit of the body (of people) ; the spirit of the group; group spirit; the morale of a group; the sense of togetherness of a group of persons; the pride, honor, and devotion of the members of a group with regard to their cause and the group as a whole; devotion to a society of which one is a member; fellowship.

(387)   est ars etiam maledicendi (L.)

There is art even in speaking evil; i.e., in reviling, slandering, etc.

(388)   esto quod esse videris (L.)

Be what you appear to be; be yourself.

(389)   et alii (fem. et aliae) (L.)

And others. Abbr. *et al.*

(390)   et cetera (L.)

And others (of similar kind) ; and so on; and so forth; and the rest or remaining.

(391)   et hoc genus omne (L.)

And all this sort (of thing) ; and all of this kind.

(392) *et semel emissum volat irrevocabile verbum (L.)*

And once emitted (uttered), a word flies irrevocably (away).

(393) *et sequens (L.)*

And the following.

(394) *et tu, Brute! (L.)*

And you (too), Brutus!—an exclamation attributed to Caesar on seeing Brutus among his assassins; hence, an outcry of reproach to a betraying friend.

(395) *États Unis d'Amérique (F.)*

The United States of America.

(396) *etiam capillus unus habet umbram suam (L.)*

Even one hair has its shadow; even a mild influence has its effect.

(397) *etiam sanato vulnere cicatrix manet (L.)*

And even when a wound is healed the scar remains.

(398) *étude (F.)*

A study (as in music); a practice piece; an exercise. Also, a musical composition, esp. one played for its artistic value.

(399) *eureka! (Gr.)*

I have found (it)!—an exclamation believed to have been uttered by Archimedes when he thought of using the principle of specific gravity in determining the purity of gold; I have got it!—an exclamation of triumph on discovering or finding something.

(400)   eventus stultorum magister (L.)

The result (of an action) is the instructor of fools;
fools learn only from experience.

(401)   ex abusu non arguitur ad usum (L.)

From abuse one does not argue against use; abuse is
no argument against sensible use.

(402)   ex accidenti (L.)

Through an accident; because of an accident; as an
accident; accidentally.

(403)   ex aequo et bono (L.)

In accordance with what is fair and good.

(404)   ex auribus cognoscitur asinus (L.)

An ass is recognized by his ears; a fool is known by
his remarks.

(405)   ex desuetudine amittuntur privilegia (L.)

Privileges are lost through disuse; special rights or
advantages or forfeited when not exercised.

(406)   ex dono dei (L.)

By the gift of God; by the grace of God.

(407)   ex fide fortis (L.)

Strong through faith; courageous because of faith.

(408)   ex libris (L.)

From the books of (the person named); from the
library of.

(409) ex mera gratia (L.)

From mere graciousness; by mere kindness; by mere favor;—rather than by obligation or the law.

(410) ex necessitate (L.)

From necessity; by reason of requirement or need.

(411) ex officio (L.)

From office; by reason of office; by virtue of one's position.

(412) ex ore parvulorum veritas (L.)

Out of the mouth of babes (comes the) truth.

(413) ex post facto (L.)

From something done afterwards; by reason of something done after a particular event; done after some event, but retroactive with reference to it; made after a thing, but having retroactive effect.

(414) ex re nata (L.)

According to the case that has arisen; in accordance with the circumstances; as the situation demands.

(415) ex tempore (L.)

Out of the moment (or time); i.e., without previous thought or preparation; extemporaneous; offhand; on the spur of the moment;—said esp. of a speech.

(416) ex umbra in solem (L.)

From shadow into the sun (sunlight); from obscurity into the spotlight; from infamy to honor.

(417) ex vitio alterius, sapiens emendat suum (L.)

From the fault of another, the wise man emends his own (error) ; a wise person learns from the mistakes of others.

(418) excelsior (L.)

Higher; still higher; ever upward;—a term used as a motto.

(419) exceptio probat regulam (L.)

The exception proves the rule.

(420) exemplo plus quam ratione vivimus (L.)

We live more by example (i.e., example set by others) than by reason.

(421) exigeant (fem. exigeante) (F.)

Fastidious; exacting; hard to please; unreasonably particular; very critical.

(422) exitus acta probat (L.)

The result proves the acts; the outcome justifies the deed; the end justifies the means.

(423) experimentum crucis (L.)

A crucial experiment; a decisive or critical test.

(424) expressis verbis (L.)

In express words; in explicit terms.

(425) extinctus amabitur idem (L.)

When dead, the same man will be loved (who is now disliked) ; i.e., quite often, the man who is disliked, or even hated, while he is living will be loved after his death.

F

(426) faber est quisque fortunae suae (L.)

Every person is the maker (designer) of his own fortune; every person is responsible for what he makes of
himself; our fates are in our own hands.

(427) fable convenue (F.)

An agreed-upon fable;—said to have been used by Voltaire in describing recorded history, which he obviously
disbelieved; a convenient myth; a piece of fiction accepted
by common consent to explain something that would
otherwise be bothersome; an accepted piece of nonsense.

(428) facile est inventis addere (L.)

It is easy to add to that which has already been invented; it is easier to improve than to invent; it is easy
to criticize that which another has created.

(429) facta, non verba (L.)

Deeds, not words; let's have action, not words.

(430) facta sunt potentiora verbis (L.)

Deeds are stronger than words; action speaks louder
than words.

(431) factum est (L.)

It is done; it is accomplished; it is finished.

(432) fait accompli (F.)

An accomplished fact; something that has already been done;—so that any discussion as to whether or not it *should* be done is pointless.

(433) fallacia alia aliam trudit (L.)

One deceit impels another; one transgression follows close upon another.

(434) falsus in uno, falsus in omnibus (L.)

False in one matter, false in all else; undependable in one thing, undependable in everything.

(435) fama nihil est celerius (L.)

Nothing is faster than a rumor; nothing travels faster than gossip.

(436) fama semper vivat! (L.)

May (his or her) fame live forever!

(437) faux pas (F.)

A false step; a blunder in social manners; a blunder in judgment; an error on a point of etiquette; a tactless observation; an undiplomatic remark.

(438) felicitas multos habet amicos (L.)

Good fortune has many friends; prosperity has many followers; a successful man has many pals.

(439) felix qui nihil debet (L.)

Happy is he who owes nothing; he who has no obligations is a happy man.

(440) *femme de lettres (F.)*

A woman of letters; a learned woman; a literary woman.

(441) *femme savante (F.)*

A learned woman; a literary woman; a bluestocking.

(442) *ferto, fereris (L.)*

Bear, and you shall be borne with; be patient with others, and others will be patient with you.

(443) *festina lente (L.)*

Hurry slowly; hurry, with deliberation; make haste slowly.

(444) *fête (F.)*

A festival; a feast; a celebration; a festive occasion.

(445) *feu sacré (F.)*

Sacred fire; divine fire; divine inspiration; ardor or eagerness divinely inspired.

(446) *fi donc! (F.)*

Fie! Fie on you! Shame on you! For shame!

(447) *fiat confirmatio (L.)*

Let confirmation be made; let it be confirmed or established.

(448) *fiat experimentum in corpore vili (L.)*

Let the experiment be made on a common (worthless) body; let the tests be made on paltry objects.

(449) *fiat justitia, ruat caelum (L.)*

Let justice be done, though the heavens tumble.

(450) *fiat justitia, ruat mundus (L.)*

Let justice be done, though the earth crashes.

(451) *fiat lux! (L.)*

Let there be light!

(452) *fiat voluntas tua! (L.)*

Thy will be done!

(453) *fide, non armis (L.)*

By faith, not by arms; by negotiation, not by warfare.

(454) *fide, sed cui vide (L.)*

Trust, but watch whom (you trust); be careful whom you trust.

(455) *fidelis ad urnam (L.)*

Faithful to the urn (of ashes); faithful unto death.

(456) *fidem qui perdit nihil ultra perdere potest (L.)*

He who loses trust can lose nothing further; he who loses faith has nothing more to lose; he who loses credit can lose no more; he who loses confidence has lost everything.

(457) *fiesta (Sp.)*

A festival; a feast; a celebration; a day of festivity; a holiday; a day of rest from regular work.

(458) *filius nullius (L.)*

The son of nobody (known) ; an illegitimate child; a bastard.

(459) *finem respice (L.)*

Look to the end; consider the end; be mindful of the outcome.

(460) *finis (L.)*

The end; it is the end; it is all over.

(461) *finis coronat opus (L.)*

The end (completion) crowns the work.

(462) *finis ecce laborum! (L.)*

Behold the end of our labors! The end of our labors is in sight!

(463) *fit fabricando faber (L.)*

The workman is made through working; working makes the craftsman; practice makes the expert; practice makes perfect.

(464) *flux de bouche (F.)*

A flow from the mouth; lalorrhea; an abnormal flow of words; excessive talk; words as opposed to action; just talk; incredible or fantastic talk.

(465) *folio recto (L.)*

On the right-hand page (of a book, manuscript, etc.) ; on the front side of the leaf (of a book, manuscript, etc.).

(466) *folio verso (L.)*

On the left-hand page (of a book, manuscript, etc.) ; on the back side of a leaf, as of a book, manuscript, etc.

(467) *forsan et haec olim meminisse juvabit (L.)*

Perhaps it will be pleasant some day to reminisce even about these things.

(468) *frangas, non flectes (L.)*

You may break, (but) you shall not bend (me).

(469) *fronti nulla fides (L.)*

There is no relying on appearance; no trust should be placed on appearance.

(470) *fructu non foliis arborem aestima (L.)*

Judge a tree by its fruit, not by its leaves.

(471) *fugit hora (L.)*

The hour flies; time flies; it is getting late.

(472) *furor loquendi (L.)*

A rage for speaking; a frenzy for making speeches.

(473) *furor scribendi (L.)*

A frenzy for writing; a frantic outburst of writing.

(474) galant homme (F.)

A man of honor; a man of his word.

(475) gauche (F.)

Left-handed; clumsy; awkward; lacking in manners; crude; without social graces; philistine.

(476) gens de lettres (F.)

Men of letters; literary persons; writers; authors; litterateurs.

(477) gens de même farine (F.)

Persons of the same flour; persons made of the same dough; birds of a feather.

(478) gens de plume (F.)

Persons of the pen; men who live by the pen; authors; writers.

(479) genus homo (L.)

Man; mankind; the species that is man; the animal that is man;—used more often in jest.

(480)   *Gesundheit! (G.)*

Health! To your health!—said esp. to a person who has just sneezed, to avert, as it were, the possibility of his coming down with a cold.

(481)   *gnothi seauton (Gr.)*

Know thyself; take stock of yourself.

(482)   *Gott sei Dank! (G.)*

Thank God! The Lord be praised! Thank goodness!

(483)   *Götterdämmerung (G.)*

1. The twilight of the gods. 2. In Germanic mythlogy, the war between the gods and their enemies; also, the time thereof. 3. The end of the world.

(484)   *grâce à Dieu (F.)*

Thanks to God; thank the Lord.

(485)   *gracias (Sp.)*

Thank you; thanks.

(486)   *grand bien vous fasse! (F.)*

May it do you much good! May it be of good omen to you!

(487)   *grand prix (F.)*

A great prize; the grand prize; the most valued prize.

(488)   *gratia gratiam parit (L.)*

(One) favor sires (another) favor; one good turn deserves another.

(489)   *graviora manent (L.)*

More serious matters (still) remain; more grievous matters remain.

(490)   *graviora quaedam sunt remedia periculis (L.)*

Some remedies are graver than the perils (they are intended to avert) ; some treatments are worse than the diseases they are supposed to cure.

(491)   *grex venalium (L.)*

A bunch of hirelings; a band of mercenaries.

(492)   *grosse tête, peu de sens (F.)*

Big head, little sense; big skull, no brains.

(493)   *guerre à mort (F.)*

War unto death; a fight to the bitter end.

(494)   *guerre de plume (F.)*

A war of the pen; an epistolary war; a war by means of the written word.

(495)   habeas corpus (L.)

Have the body (i.e., bring the person before a judge);
—the name of an order requiring the proper authorities
to bring a specified prisoner into court before a judge,
at a stated time and place, to determine the legality of his
detention.

(496)   habent sua fata libelli (L.)

(Even) pamphlets have their own fate; writings have
their own destiny; books have their own peculiar fortunes.

(497)   haec olim meminisse juvabit (L.)

Someday it will be pleasant to remember these things.

(498)   heareticus in grammatica (L.)

A heretic in matters of grammar; an iconoclast in
grammar.

(499)   hasta la vista (Sp.)

Until the (next) seeing; until the next meeting; until
we see each other again; good-by; farewell.

(500)   hasta mañana (Sp.)

Until tomorrow; good-by.

(501) *hatti-sherif (Turk.)*

An irrevocable decision; an irrevocable order;—in allusion to a Turkish decree which could not be revoked when signed by a sultan.

(502) *haut à la main (F.)*

High with the hand; highhanded; overbearing; arrogant; arbitrary.

(503) *heluo librorum (L.)*

A glutton for books; one who gormandizes books; a bookworm; an avid reader. Also spelled *helluo librorum*.

(504) *hiatus valde deflendus (L.)*

An interval much to be deplored; a gap greatly to be lamented.

(505) *hic et nunc (L.)*

Here and now; forthwith; at once.

(506) *hic funis nihil attraxit (L.)*

This line has attracted nothing; this venture has yielded nothing; this attempt ended in failure; this try was for nothing.

(507) *hoc opus, hic labor est (L.)*

This is (really) work, this is labor; i.e., this is really the tough part of the job; this is really hard work.

(508) *hoc titulo (L.)*

By this title; under this title; under this name.

(509) *homme de lettres (F.)*

A man of letters; a man who appreciates literature; a literary man; a writer of literary works.

(510) homme de plume (F.)

A man of the pen; a man who lives by the pen, i.e., by writing; an author.

(511) homo multarum litterarum (L.)

A man of much education or learning.

(512) honneur et patrie (F.)

Honor and country;—a motto of the French Legion of Honor.

(513) honoris causa (L.)

For honor's sake; for the sake of honoring, as in conferring an honorary degree.

(514) hors d'oeuvre (F.)

Outside the work; outside the main work; outside the subject; something extra; something unusual.

(515) hors d'oeuvres (F.)

Outside the works; outside the main dish; an appetizer or a light dish served at the beginning of a meal, as anchovies, olives, etc.

(516) hôtel-Dieu (F.)

Hotel (or house) of God; a hospital; esp. the main hospital of a town. Also written *l'hôtel-Dieu*.

(517) humanum est errare (L.)

It is human to err; to err is human.

(518) hunc tu caveto (L.)

Beware thou of him; beware of that man.

I

(519) iacta alea est (L.)

The die is cast; the decision is made.

(520) ibi semper est victoria ubi concordia est (L.)

Victory is always there where concord is; victory is found where there is harmony; there is strength in unity.

(521) ibidem (L.)

In the same place;—generally referring to a source of citation indicated previously;—usually written in the abbreviated form *ibid.*

(522) idem (L.)

The same; the same as that mentioned previously.

(523) idem quod (L.)

The same as (that mentioned before).

(524) ignorantia legis neminem excusat (L.)

Ignorance of the law excuses no one.

(525) illotis manibus (L.)

With unwashed hands; with unclean hands; without the necessary preparatory measures; with the galligaskins down.

(526)   imitatores, servum pecus! (L.)

Imitators, a servile pack!

(527)   immedicabile vulnus (L.)

An irremediable wound; an incurable trauma.

(528)   imprimatur (L.)

Let it be printed;—an official license by a civil or religious authority for the printing or publishing of a paper, pamphlet, book, journal, etc.; an official approval of a published work. Also, in general, a permit, a sanction, etc.

(529)   imprimerie (F.)

A printing plant; a printing office; printing.

(530)   in absentia (L.)

In (the) absence; during the absence; in spite of one's absence;—used esp. with reference to a person who is honored, judged, or tried during his absence.

(531)   in abstracto (L.)

In the abstract; regarded apart from any particular case.

(532)   in aedibus (L.)

In the house of; at the house of;—used, formerly, with reference to printing houses.

(533)   in aequilibrio (L.)

In equilibrium; in balance; in harmony.

(534)   in aeternum (L.)

Forever; always; eternally; everlastingly.

(535)   in ambiguo (L.)

In ambiguity; in doubt; in obscurity; in uncertainty; vaguely; indefinitely.

(536)   in aqua scribis (L.)

You are writing in water; you are wasting your time.

(537)   in arduis virtus (L.)

Virtue in trouble; virtue in difficulties.

(538)   in Dei nomine (L.)

In the name of God; for God's sake.

(539)   in Deo speramus (L.)

In God we hope; in God we lay our hope.

(540)   in diem vivere (L.)

To live for the day; to live for the present; to live without regard for the future; to live from day to day.

(541)   in dubiis (L.)

In doubtful situations; in uncertain matters; in undecided issues.

(542)   in dubio (L.)

In doubt; uncertain; not determined.

(543)   in excelsis (L.)

In the highest (degree) ; on high.

(544)   in extenso (L.)

In extended form; at length; in full.

(545)   in hoc (L.)

In this; in this respect; as to this matter.

(546)   in infinitum (L.)

In infinity; in the realm of the infinite; in the endlessness of time and/or space. Also, to infinity.

(547)   in manus tuas (L.)

Into thy hands; in your care.

(548)   in memoriam (L.)

In memory (of) ; to the memory (of) ;—a phrase used in epitaphs and other mementos of the deceased.

(549)   in nomine (L.)

In the name of (the person specified).

(550)   in nomine Dei (L.)

In the name of God; for God's sake.

(551)   in nomine Domini (L.)

In the name of the Lord.

(552)   in omnia paratus (L.)

In all things prepared; ready for all eventualities; ready for anything.

(553)   in perpetuum (L.)

In perpetuity; for eternity; forever.

(554)   in perpetuam rei memoriam (L.)

In perpetual memory of the thing; in everlasting memory of the affair.

(555)   *in potentia (L.)*

In potential; potentially; in a state of possibility; in a condition of having the ability.

(556)   *in saecula saeculorum (L.)*

For ages of ages; for ages and ages; forever and ever.

(557)   *in situ (L.)*

In the site; in position; in the original place where normally found; in the place found, whether normal or abnormal;—often used to designate an organ in its natural location.

(558)   *in statu quo (L.)*

In the state in which; i.e., in the state in which the thing or situation spoken of is or was at a specified time; in the same state as before.

(559)   *in testimonium (L.)*

In testimony; in witness.

(560)   *in toto (L.)*

In the whole; all together; as a unit; as one.

(561)   *in utero (L.)*

In the uterus; in the womb; i.e., unborn.

(562)   *in vitro (L.)*

In glass; in the test tube; in an experimental environment, as opposed to the natural (*in vivo*).

(563)   in vivo (L.)

In the living body; in the living organism;—used esp. with regard to biological processes, physiological or experimental, taking place in the living animal, as opposed to the test tube or other experimental environment (*in vitro*).

(564)   injuria non excusat injuriam (L.)

One wrong does not excuse (justify) another wrong.

(565)   inquisitio post mortem (L.)

A post-mortem inquest; an inquest conducted after the death of a person.

(566)   integros haurire fontes (L.)

To draw water from unpolluted fountains; to draw knowledge from fresh and authoritative sources; to learn from upright teachers.

(567)   intellige ut credas (L.)

Understand so that you may believe.

(568)   intelligenti pauca (L.)

For the intelligent few (words are sufficient) ; a word to the wise is sufficient.

(569)   inter folia fructus (L.)

Between the leaves the fruit; the meaning is between the lines.

(570)   intra muros (L.)

Within the walls;—said esp. with reference to a city or the domain of a college.

(571) *ipse dixit (L.)*

He himself has said (it) ;—an implication that the statement is not proved; a dogmatic assertion.

(572) *ipso facto (L.)*

By the fact itself; by the act itself; by the very nature of the fact; by the mere fact.

J

(573) jawohl (G.)

Yes indeed; quite so; certainly; to be sure; of course.

(574) jacta alea est (L.)

The die is cast;—a saying attributed to Julius Caesar on the occasion of his crossing the Rubicon which started a civil war.

(575) Jahre lehren mehr als Bücher (G.)

The years teach more than books; experience is a better teacher than books.

(576) je crains que cela ne soit (F.)

I fear that it is so; I fear that this is true.

(577) jeu de mots (F.)

A play of words; a play on words; a pun.

(578) joie de vivre (F.)

The joy of living; keen enjoyment of life; the relish of the pleasures of life; the zest for life and its joys.

(579) jucunda rerum vicissitudo (L.)

An agreeable change of circumstances; a pleasant change in the course of events; a joyful change of luck.

(580)   *jucundi acti labores (L.)*

Accomplished labors are pleasant; sweet is the work that is finished.

(581)   *judicium capitale (L.)*

Capital judgment; a judgment of death; a sentence of death.

(582)   *judicium Dei (L.)*

The judgment of God; divine judgment.

(583)   *jura naturae sunt immutabilia (L.)*

The laws of nature are unalterable.

(584)   *juris peritus (L.)*

Experienced in the law; expert in the law; well versed in the law.

(585)   *jus canonicum (L.)*

The canon law; the law governing the religious affairs of a Christian church.

(586)   *jus civile (L.)*

Civil law; the law dealing with private rights.

(587)   *jus ex injuria non oritur (L.)*

Right does not rise out of a wrong.

(588)   *jus naturale (L.)*

A law of nature; a natural law.

(589)   *jus scriptum (L.)*

The written law; i.e., the body of laws created by legislation or enactment, as opposed to the unwritten or common law.

(590)   *justa causa (L.)*

A just cause; a righteous cause.

(591) *Kürze ist der Rede Würze (G.)*

Brevity is the root of speech; brevity is the essence of a good oration; brevity is the soul of wit.

(592)   *la maladie sans maladie (F.)*

The disease without disease; the disease without an organic disease; hypochondria; mental depression; any functional mental disease.

(593)   *la verità è figlia del tempo (It.)*

Truth is the daughter of time; the truth will out in time.

(594)   *laisser faire (F.)*

Same as *laissez faire,* i.e., a policy of noninterference; a hands-off policy by the government with regard to business, labor-industry relations, etc.

(595)   *laissez faire (F.)*

Let (people) do (as they please) ; a policy of non-interference; a policy of letting business owners set their own rules of competition, without interference by the government; a hands-off policy by the government of a country with regard to labor-industry relations.

(596)   *laudum immensa cupido (L.)*

An endless desire for praise.

(597)   *le roi est mort, vive le roi! (F.)*

The king is dead, long live the king!

(598) *lege totum si vis scire totum (L.)*

Read all if you wish to know all; read the whole if you wish to know the whole.

(599) *les misérables (F.)*

The unfortunate ones; the outcasts; the wretched; the destitute.

(600) *lex non scripta (L.)*

The unwritten law; esp., the common law.

(601) *liberavi animam meam (L.)*

I have freed my soul; I have unburdened my mind.

(602) *liberum arbitrium (L.)*

Free choice; free will.

(603) *licentia vatum (L.)*

The license of poets; poetic license; an artist's right to deviate from strict rules, to achieve greater effect.

(604) *limbus fatuorum (L.)*

The limbo of fools; the abode of fools; a fools' paradise.

(605) *lis litem generat (L.)*

Controversy generates controversy; dispute begets dispute.

(606) *litem lite resolvere (L.)*

To resolve dispute by dispute; to settle one difficulty by creating another.

(607)   *literatim* (L.)
Literally; to the letter; letter for letter.

(608)   *littera scripta manet* (L.)
The written letter remains; the written word lasts.

(609)   *litterae scriptae manent* (L.)
Written letters remain; written words last.

(610)   *loco citato* (L.)
In the place cited; in the passage quoted

(611)   *loco primo citato* (L.)
In the place first cited.

(612)   *loco supra citato* (L.)
In the place cited above; in the above-mentioned place.

M

(613) ma chère (F.) fem.
My dear; my sweetheart.

(614) ma foi! (F.)
My faith; Upon my faith! Really! Indeed! Upon my word!

(615) macte animo (L.)
Continue in (or with) courage;—an exhortation; proceed with courage; more courage to you.

(616) macte virtute esto! (L.)
Bravo! Well done! Continue in your excellent way.

(617) magna cum laude (L.)
With great praise; with great honor; with great distinction;—a tribute used in diplomas.

(618) magna est veritas, et praevalebit (L.)
Great is the truth, and it will prevail; mighty is the truth, and it will triumph.

(619) magna est veritas, et praevalet (L.)
The truth is great, and it prevails; the truth is powerful, and it triumphs.

(620)   *magna vis est conscientiae (L.)*
Great is the strength of conscience.

(621)   *magnas inter opes inops (L.)*
Destitute in the midst of great riches.

(622)   *magnifico (Sp.)*
Magnificent; excellent; splendid; grand.

(623)   *magnifique (F.)*
Magnificent; excellent; splendid; grand.

(624)   *magnum opus (L.)*
A great work; the great work; one's best work.

(625)   *maison de santé (F.)*
A house of health; a private hospital; a private sanatorium.

(626)   *majori cedo (L.)*
I give up to a superior; I yield to my better.

(627)   *male narrando fabula depravatur (L.)*
By badly narrating, a story is spoiled.

(628)   *mater artium necessitas (L.)*
Necessity is the mother of invention.

(629)   *materiem superabat opus (L.)*
The workmanship excelled the material.

(630)   *maxima cum laude (L.)*
With the greatest praise; with the greatest distinction.

(631)   maximum remedium irae mora est (L.)

The greatest remedy for anger is a delay (or pause).

(632)   maximus novator tempus (L.)

Time is the greatest changer of things (i.e., innovator).

(633)   media in vitae in morte sumus (L.)

In the midst of life we are in death; in the midst of our activities death claims us.

(634)   medice, cura teipsum (L.)

Physician, heal thyself; put your own house in order first.

(635)   medicus curat, natura sanat (L.)

The physician cares for (the patient), nature makes (him) well.

(636)   meglio tardi che mai (It.)

Better late than never.

(637)   melioribus annis (L.)

In better years; in happier years or times.

(638)   memor et fidelis (L.)

Mindful (remembering) and faithful.

(639)   memorabile nomen (L.)

A remarkable name; a memorable name; a name worth remembering.

(640)   memorabilia (L.)

Things worthy of remembrance; things worth recording; notable events.

(641)　*memoria in aeterna (L.)*

In eternal memory (or remembrance).

(642)　*mens aequa in arduis (L.)*

A well-balanced mind in arduous circumstances; a level head in a difficult situation; a cool head in trying times.

(643)　*mens sana in corpore sano (L.)*

A sound mind in a healthy body; a double blessing.

(644)　*meo periculo (L.)*

At my own risk; at my own hazard.

(645)　*meshummad (Heb.)*

A Jew converted to Christianity; an apostate from Judaism; any apostate or renegade.

(646)　*mihi cura futuri (L.)*

My anxiety is for the future.

(647)　*minatur innocentibus qui parcit nocentibus (L.)*

He who spares the guilty threatens the innocent.

(648)　*minima de malis (L.)*

The least of evils; of evils choose the least.

(649)　*mitis sapientia (L.)*

Mature wisdom; seasoned discretion; mellowed good judgment.

(650)　*mitius imperanti melius paretur (L.)*

The more gently one commands, the better he is complied with.

(651)   mitte hanc de pectore curam (L.)

Dismiss this anxiety from your breast; dismiss this care from your heart.

(652)   modus omnibus in rebus (L.)

Moderation in all things; the proper measure in all things.

(653)   molliter ossa cubent (L.)

May the bones lie undisturbed; may his bones rest in peace.

(654)   mon Dieu! (F)

My God! Good Heavens!

(655)   monde savant (F.)

The learned world; the well-informed world; the world of science.

(656)   monstrum horrendum (L.)

A horrible monster; a frightful ogre.

(657)   monumentum aere perennius (L.)

A monument more lasting than bronze; an enduring monument; an everlasting memorial.

(658)   more probato (L.)

In the tried manner; in the approved manner.

(659)   Morgenstunde hat Gold im Munde (G.)

1. The morning hour has gold in its mouth; the early hours are auspicious ones; the early morning hours favor every kind of undertaking. 2. The early bird catches the worm; early to bed and early to rise makes a man healthy, wealthy, and wise.

(660)   *mors omnia solvit (L.)*

Death solves all things; death dissolves all things; death resolves all difficulties; death takes care of everything.

(661)   *mors omnibus communis (L.)*

Death is common to all; everyone must die.

(662)   *mors ultima ratio (L.)*

Death is the last reckoning; death is the last transaction; death is the last argument.

(663)   *mortuo leoni et lepores insultant (L.)*

A dead lion is insulted even by (the timid) hares.

(664)   *motos praestat componere fluctus (L.)*

It is advisable to quiet turbulent waters.

(665)   *mucho en el suelo, poco en el cielo (Sp.)*

Much on this earth, little in heaven.

(666)   *multa gemens (L.)*

Sighing much; groaning much; grumbling much.

(667)   *multa paucis (L.)*

Much in few (words) ; a great deal of significance in a few words; the saying of much with few words.

(668)   *multis ictibus dejicitur quercus (L.)*

(Even) an oak is felled by many blows; even a strong man has a limit for his endurance.

(669)   *mundus vult decipi (L.)*

The world likes to be beguiled; the world wishes to be deceived.

(670) *natura appetit perfectum* (L.)

Nature strives for perfection.

(671) *natura non facit saltum* (L.)

Nature does not make a jump; nature does not leap; nature makes no sudden changes.

(672) *naufragium in portu facere* (L.)

1. To have or suffer a shipwreck in port; to come a cropper while on the verge of success; to fail with the end in sight; to come to naught after a long series of successes. 2. To fail even before one gets a good start; to come to ruin at the very beginning.

(673) *ne cede malis* (L.)

Do not yield to misfortune; don't give up the ship.

(674) *ne fronti crede* (L.)

Do not trust the external quality; do not rely on appearances.

(675) *ne prius antidotum quam venenum* (L.)

(Do) not (take) the antidote before the poison; don't anticipate trouble; do first things first; don't be in an excessive hurry.

(676)   ne puero gladium (L.)

(Give) not a sword to a boy; do not entrust a boy with a dangerous weapon; don't give a man's job to a boy.

(677)   ne quid nimis (L.)

Nothing to excess; nothing too much; let there be no excess; be moderate.

(678)   ne tentes, aut perfice (L.)

Don't attempt, or finish; don't start unless you mean to finish.

(679)   nec habeo, nec careo, nec curo (L.)

I have not, I desire not, I care not.

(680)   nec prece nec pretio (L.)

Neither by prayer (i.e., entreaty) nor by bribe; neither for love nor for money.

(681)   nec quaerere nec spernere honorem (L.)

Neither to seek honor nor to spurn it.

(682)   neiges d'antan (F.)

Snows of yesteryear; water under the bridge; things of the past.

(683)   nemine dissentiente (L.)

No one dissenting; without a dissenting vote or voice; unanimously.

(684)   nemo cogitationis poenam patitur (L.)

No one suffers punishment because of his thoughts.

(685) nemo dat quod non habet (L.)

No one gives what he does not have; i.e., no one can give away that which he does not own.

(686) nemo solus satis sapit (L.)

No one is wise enough all by himself.

(687) nervus probandi (L.)

The sinew of proof; the "nerve" of the proof; the substance of the proof; the main argument.

(688) n'est-ce pas? (F.)

Isn't it so? Isn't that so?

(689) nicht wahr? (G.)

Isn't it true? Not true? Isn't it so?

(690) nihil ex nihilo (L.)

Nothing from nothing; nothing comes from nothing.

(691) nihil praeferendum honestati (L.)

Nothing must be placed before honor.

(692) nihil quod tetigit non ornavit (L.)

Nothing that he touched he did not adorn; he adorned everything that he touched.

(693) nil admirari (L.)

To admire nothing; to wonder at nothing; to be astonished by nothing; to be moved by nothing. Hence, an attitude of indifference.

(694) nil agit exemplum litem quod lite resolvit (L.)

An example which settles dispute by dispute accomplishes nothing; an example which resolves one difficulty by introducing another accomplishes nothing.

(695) nil desperandum (L.)

Nothing must be despaired of; never give up; never despair.

(696) nitor in adversum (L.)

I press forward against opposition.

(697) no es oro todo que reluce (Sp.)

Not all that glitters is gold; all that glitters is not gold.

(698) noblesse oblige (F.)

Nobility obliges; rank involves responsibility; social position imposes obligations, as of magnanimity; people of high rank should behave nobly and be charitable toward others who are less fortunate.

(699) nolo contendere (L.)

I do not wish to contest; a plea by a defendant in a criminal case stating that, without admitting guilt, he will not make a defense.

(700) nom de guerre (F.)

A war name; a battle name; an assumed name; a pseudonym.

(701) nom de plume (F.)

A pen name; an assumed name; a pseudonym; an assumed name used by an author.

(702) *non capisco (It.)*
I do not understand.

(703) *non compos mentis (L.)*
Not of sound mind; not qualified mentally to handle one's affairs.

(704) *non culpabilis (L.)*
Not guilty; not blameable; not to be reproached.

(705) *non est fumus absque igne (L.)*
There is no smoke without fire.

(706) *non est vivere sed valere vita est (L.)*
Living is not being (merely) alive but being well.

(707) *non nobis solum (L.)*
Not for us only; not for ourselves alone.

(708) *non omnis moriar (L.)*
I shall not die wholly (or entirely); not all of me shall die; something of me shall survive (as in the form of a book, painting, etc.).

(709) *non progredi est regredi (L.)*
Not to go ahead is to go backward; not to progress is to regress.

(710) *non quis sed quid (L.)*
(The question is) not who but what.

(711) *non quo sed quomodo (L.)*
(The question is) not by whom but how.

(712)　non sequitur (L.)

It does not follow;—said esp. of a conclusion not logically related to the premises.

(713)　non sibi sed omnibus (L.)

Not for oneself but for all.

(714)　non sum qualis eram (L.)

I am not of the kind I was; I am not what I used to be; I am not the man I used to be.

(715)　non tali auxilio nec defensoribus istis tempus eget (L.)

Not for such aid or for such defenders does this situation call.

(716)　nondum editus (L.)

Not yet put forth; not yet published.

(717)　nondum omnium dierum sol occidit (L.)

The sun has not yet set for all days; all hope is not gone; there will be another day.

(718)　nosce te ipsum (L.)

Know thyself; know yourself first.

(719)　notabilia (L.)

Things worth noting; things worth observing and remembering.

(720)　notanda (L.)

Things that should be noted; things that should be observed and remembered.

(721)   nous poietikos (Gr.)

Creative mind; creative or active reason.

(722)   nous verrons (F.)

We shall see; we shall find out.

(723)   nous verrons ce que nous verrons (F.)

We shall see what we shall see.

(724)   nulla dies sine linea (L.)

No day without a line;—i.e., no day shall pass without the addition of a line to one's writing.

(725)   nulla nuova, buona nuova (It.)

No news (is) good news.

(726)   nulla regula sine exceptione (L.)

No rule (is) without an exception; every rule has an exception.

(727)   nunc aut nunquam (L.)

Now or never; now or not at all.

(728)   O si sic omnia! (L.)

Oh, if all were thus! If things were so!

(729)   O tempora! O mores! (L.)

Oh the times! Oh the manners! How the manners change with the times!

(730)   obscurum per obscurius (L.)

An obscure thing by the more obscure; the explaining of somthing obscure in terms that are even more obscure.

(731)   odium medicum (L.)

Medical hatred; hatred among physicians.

(732)   odium theologicum (L.)

Theological hatred; hatred or enmity among theologians.

(733)   omnem movere lapidem (L.)

To move every stone; to make every effort; to leave no stone unturned.

(734)   omnia ad Dei gloriam (L.)

All things are for the glory of God.

(735) omnia mutantur (L.)

All things change; time changes all things.

(736) opere citato (L.)

In the work quoted; in the work cited.

(737) opprobrium medicorum (L.)

The disgrace of physicians; i.e., any disease for which physicians have no remedy.

(738) ora e sempre (It.)

Now and always; now and forever.

(739) orbis scientiarum (L.)

The circle of the sciences; the sum of scientific knowledge.

(740) otia dant vitia (L.)

Idleness gives vices; leisure breeds depravity.

(741) otiosa sedulitas (L.)

Leisurely assiduity; quiet diligence.

(742) oublier je ne puis (F.)

I am unable to forget.

(743) pacta sunt servanda (L.)

Pacts are to be kept (observed); agreements should be honored.

(744) palmam qui meruit ferat (L.)

Let him carry away the palm who has deserved it; let him who deserved it get the honor (reward).

(745) par excellence (F.)

By way of excellence; in the highest degree of excellence; pre-eminently; above all others; beyond comparison.

(746) parva leves capiunt animas (L.)

Small matters occupy light minds; trifling matters occupy small minds.

(747) pas à pas on va bien loin (F.)

Step by step one goes quite far;—i.e., perseverance even at a slow rate brings results.

(748) patience passe science (F.)

Patience surpasses (i.e., is superior to) science; patience achieves more than knowledge.

(749) pax vobis (L.)

Peace to you; peace be with you.

(750) pax vobiscum (L.)

Peace (be) with you.

(751) per ambages (L.)

In a roundabout way; with evasion; by circumlocution; in a secret way; in a mysterious manner.

(752) per angusta ad augusta (L.)

Through narrow ways (straits) to noble ends; through difficulties to splendor; through hardships to glory.

(753) per annum (L.)

By the year; for the year; for each year; annually; yearly.

(754) per ardua ad astra (L.)

Through difficulties to the stars; through adversity to the pinnacle.

(755) per aspera ad astra (L.)

Through adversities to the stars; through difficulties to the highest achievement.

(756) per se (L.)

By itself; in itself; as such; inherently.

(757) pereunt et imputantur (L.)

They pass and are reckoned; i.e., the hours and the days pass and they are scored against us;—a lugubrious reflection on the ephemeral nature of life.

(758)   periculum in mora (L.)

Danger in delay; there is peril in tardiness or procrastination.

(759)   permitte divis cetera (L.)

Entrust the rest to the gods; leave the rest to fate.

(760)   petit à petit (F.)

Little by little; gradually; by degrees.

(761)   piece de résistance (F.)

Piece of resistance; the main dish of a meal; the main feature; the principal event in a series of events.

(762)   piscem natare doces (L.)

You are teaching a fish how to swim.

(763)   pondere, non numero (L.)

By weight, not by number; by quality, not by quantity.

(764)   post meridiem (L.)

After midday; after noon.

(765)   post mortem (L.)

1. After death; occurring after death. 2. A postmortem examination; a medical examination of a human body after death, generally in order to determine the cause of death or to ascertain the condition of the body prior to death. 3. Jocosely, a delving into the causes of a failure.

(766)   post tenebras lux (L.)

After darkness (comes) light; good luck follows bad luck.

(767)   *post tot naufragia portum (L.)*

After so many shipwrecks (finally) the harbor; after
so many adversities, finally good luck.

(768)   *potius mori quam foedari (L.)*

Rather to die than to be defiled (or dishonored).

(769)   *poudre aux yeux (F.)*

Dust in the eyes; wool over the eyes; something that
diverts attention from facts; something that blinds a person to reality.

(770)   *pour encourager les autres (F.)*

To encourage the others; to serve as a stimulus for
others.

(771)   *pour faire de l'esprit (F.)*

To display one's wit; to demonstrate spirit, vitality,
etc.

(772)   *pour le mérite (F.)*

For merit; for due worth or desert.

(773)   *praemia virtutis (L.)*

The rewards of virtue; the benefits of moral excellence.

(774)   *praemonitus, praemunitius (L.)*

Forewarned (is) forearmed.

(775)   *prendre la lune avec les dents (F.)*

To grasp the moon with the teeth; to attempt to do the
impossible.

(776)   *presto maturo, presto marcio (It.)*

Quickly ripe, quickly rotten; easy come, easy go.

(777)   *prima caritas incipit a se ipso (L.)*

Charity begins first with oneself; charity begins at home.

(778)   *prima facie (L.)*

On the first face; on the first appearance; at first sight; on the face of it.

(779)   *primus in orbe deo fecit timor (L.)*

Fear first created gods in the world; fear was the first creator of gods.

(780)   *primus inter pares (L.)*

First among his equals; a spokesman for a group of peers.

(781)   *principia, non homines (L.)*

Principles, not men (count).

(782)   *principiorum non est ratio (L.)*

There is no (need for) reasoning regarding principles; principles or fundamentals need no proof.

(783)   *pro re nata (L.)*

For the thing that has arisen; for any occasion that may arise; for an emergency;—an instruction seen on prescriptions, directing the patient to take the medicine when the need for it arises.

(784)   *propositio de necessario (L.)*

A necessary proposition.

(785)   *propositio de omni (L.)*

A universal proposition; a proposition which affirms or denies something about every member of a group.

(786) proprietates verborum (L.)

The accepted standards of words; the accepted usage of words; the correct meanings of words.

(787) pulvis et umbra sumus (L.)

We are (but) dust and shadow.

(788) punctum comparationis (L.)

A point of comparison; a basis for comparison.

(789) punctum saliens (L.)

A salient point; a conspicuous point or feature; a jumping-off point; a starting point.

(790) *qua cursum ventus (L.)*
Where the wind (their) course (guides).

(791) *quae fuerunt vitia mores sunt (L.)*
The things that were (once) vices are (now) customs.

(792) *quae nocent, docent (L.)*
The things that hurt (often) teach.

(793) *quaere verum (L.)*
Seek the truth; determine the facts.

(794) *qualis pater, talis filius (L.)*
As is the father, so is the son; like father, like son.

(795) *qualis rex, talis grex (L.)*
As is the king, so are the people; as is the leader, so are the followers.

(796) *qualis vir, talis oratio (L.)*
As is the man, so is his speech; the words befit the man.

(797) *qualis vita, finis ita (L.)*
As is the life, so is the end; one dies in the same manner as one lives.

(798)   quem Deus perdere vult prius dementat (L.)

Him whom God wishes to destroy, he first makes mad (irrational or angry).

(799)   quem di diligunt adolescens moritur (L.)

He whom the gods esteem dies growing up (i.e., young) ; the good die young.

(800)   qu'en dira-t-on? (F.)

What will people say?

(801)   qui bene distinguit bene docet (L.)

He who distinguishes well teaches well; he who makes fine discriminations makes a good teacher.

(802)   qui bene interrogat bene docet (L.)

He who questions well teaches well.

(803)   qui docet discit (L.)

He who teaches (also) learns.

(804)   qui invidet minor est (L.)

He who envies is (an) inferior (person).

(805)   qui non proficit deficit (L.)

He who does not progress regresses; he who does not go forward falls behind.

(806)   qui parcit nocentibus innocentes punit (L.)

He who spares the guilty (thereby) punishes the innocent.

(807)   qui scribit bis legit (L.)

He who writes reads twice; i.e., he who writes a thing down will remember it as well as if he were to read it twice; for the memory, writing once equals reading twice.

(808)   quit sentit commodum sentire debet et onus (L.)

He who feels (enjoys) the benefit should also feel the burden.

(809)   qui s'excuse s'accuse (F.)

He who excuses himself (thereby) accuses himself (i.e., admits the existence of guilt).

(810)   qui tacet consentit (L.)

He who is silent (regarding an issue, thereby) consents (i.e., is regarded as consenting).

(811)   quid est veritas? (L.)

What is truth?—a question asked by Pilate.

(812)   quien mal dice, peor oye (Sp.)

He who speaks evil, hears (even) worse.

(813)   quién sabe? (Sp.)

Who knows? Who is able?

(814)   quis custodiet ipsos custodes? (L.)

Who shall watch the watchmen themselves!

(815)   quis, quid, ubi, quibus auxiliis, cur, quomodo, quando? (L.)

Who, what, where, by what means, why, how, when? —questions eliciting all the information regarding a case.

(816)   quo Fata vocant (L.)

Whither the Fates beckon (or call).

(817)   quo vadis? (L.)

Whither goest thou? Where are you headed for? Where are you going?

(818)   quod vide (L.)

Which see; which look up;—as a citation or reference.

(819)   quos Jupiter perdere vult prius dementat (L.)

Those whom Jupiter wishes to destroy he first makes mad (angry or irrational).

(820)   quot homines, tot sententiae (L.)

As many men, so many opinions; so many people, so many opinions.

(821) rast' ich, so rost' ich (G.)

When I rest, I rust; when I am inactive, I deteriorate.

(822) ratio decidendi (L.)

The rationale for deciding; the reason for deciding; the logic of coming to a conclusion.

(823) recueil choisi (F.)

Choice selection; elegant collection.

(824) reddite quae sunt Caesaris Caesari (L.)

Render unto Caesar the things that are Caesar's.

(825) reductio ad absurdum (L.)

1. The method of disproving a proposition by showing its results to be absurd if carried to the implied conclusion. 2. The method of proving or supporting a proposition by showing that its opposite is foolish, absurd, or impossible. 3. The method of disproving a proposition by showing its absurdity when amplified or carried to an extreme.

(826) regis ad exemplum (L.)

After the example of the king; in emulation of a distinguished person.

104

(827)   rem tene, verba sequentur (L.)

Grasp the substance, the words will follow; select a topic to speak about and the words will come to you.

(828)   répondez, s'il vous plaît (F.)

Answer, if you please;—a request for an answer in response to an invitation. Abbreviated *R.S.V.P.*

(829)   requiescat in pace (L.)

May he (or she) rest in peace.

(830) res est ingeniosa dare (L.)

It is a good thing to give; it is noble to give.

(831)   res gestae (L.)

Things done (or accomplished) ; facts; deeds; exploits. Also, in law, the facts or things which accompany or form the environment of a case.

(832)   res in cardine est (L.)

The thing is on a pivot (i.e., a turning point) ; the matter or affair is at a critical point.

(833)   respice finem (L.)

Look to the end; look at the possible outcome.

(834)   respondeat superior (L.)

Let the superior (the master) answer (for his subordinate, employee, etc.).

(835)   revenons à nos moutons (F.)

Let us return to our sheep; i.e., let us return to the subject (from which we digressed).

(836)   rien ne pèse tant qu'um secret (F.)

Nothing burdens so heavily as a secret.

(837)   rigor mortis (L.)

Stiffness of death; the rigidity which affects the muscles of the body after death.

(838)   rira bien qui rira le dernier (F.)

He who laughs last laughs best.

(839)   robur et corporis et animi (L.)

Vigor of body and of mind; physical and mental strength.

(840)   rois fainéants (F.)

Idle kings; do-nothing rulers;—applied esp. to kings having no governing powers.

(841)   ruin señor cria ruin servidor (Sp.)

A mean master makes a mean servant.

(842)   sabrer une affaire (F.)

To do a job in a careless manner; to scamp a duty.

(843)   saevis tranquillus in undis (L.)

Calm in raging waves; composed in face of excitement; serene amid turmoil.

(844)   sain de corps et d'esprit (F.)

Sound in body and mind.

(845)   salus ubi multi consiliarii (L.)

There is safety where there are many counselors.

(846)   sans peur et sans reproche (F.)

Without fear and without reproach.

(847)   sans phrase (F.)

Without affected style; without circumlocution; in plain language; to the point.

(848)   sans rime et sans raison (F.)

Without rhyme and reason; without a plan and without justification.

(849)   sans souci (F.)

Without care; without worry; gay; carefree; freedom from care; an informal gathering.

(850)   *sapere aude (L.)*

To dare to be wise; to dare to be sensible; to dare to be discreet.

(851)   *sapiens qui prospicit (L.)*

He who looks forward is wise.

(852)   *satis eloquentiae, sapientiae parum (L.)*

Enough of eloquence (but) too little of wisdom.

(853)   *satis superque (L.)*

Enough and beyond; enough and more than enough; enough and to spare; plenty; more than enough.

(854)   *Schuster, bleib' bei deinem Leisten (G.)*

Cobbler, stick to your last; let no one venture into a field in which he is not qualified; let everyone stick to his own province.

(855)   *scientia intuitiva (L.)*

Intuitive knowledge; intuitive understanding.

(856)   *scriptor classicus (L.)*

A classical writer; an author who writes for the elite; a writer for selected readers.

(857)   *se non è vero, è ben trovato (It.)*

If it is not true, it is well contrived.

(858)   *secret de la comédie (F.)*

Everybody's secret; an open secret.

(859)   *secundum aequm et bonum (L.)*

According to what is equitable and right.

(860) secundum bonos mores (L.)

According to good practices; according to accepted custom.

(861) semitae sapientiae (L.)

The footpaths of wisdom; the byways of wisdom.

(862) semper fidelis (L.)

Always faithful;—the motto of the United States Marine Corps.

(863) semper timidum scelus (L.)

A guilty person is always timid; guilt is always timid.

(864) sermo index animo (L.)

Speech (is) the index of the mind.

(865) sero venientibus ossa (L.)

For those who come late, (nothing but) the bones (or leftovers).

(866) serus in caelum redeas (L.)

May you return to heaven late; i.e., may you live long.

(867) servabo fidem (L.)

I will observe the faith; I will keep faith.

(868) sesquipedalia verba (L.)

Words a foot and a half long; long words; polysyllabic words.

(869) si c'est possible, c'est fait; si c'est impossible, cela se fera (F.)

If it is possible, it is (already, or as good as,) done; if it is impossible, it shall be done (nevertheless).

(870)   si Deus pro nobis, quis contra nos? (L.)

If God be for us, who shall be against us?

(871)   si hic esses, aliter sentires (L.)

If you were here, you would feel otherwise; if you were in this (my, his, etc.) situation, you would have another opinion.

(872)   si jeunesse savait, si viellesse pouvait! (F.)

If youth knew, if old age were able! If youth had the knowledge of old age and old age had the ability of youth.

(873)   si parva licet componere magnis (L.)

If it is permitted to compare small things with great; —used esp. as introductory to such a comparison.

(874)   si post fata venit gloria, non propero (L.)

If glory comes after death, I do not hurry (i.e., I am in no hurry for the glory).

(875)   sic eunt fata hominum (L.)

So go the fates (fortunes) of men.

(876)   sic itur ad astra (L.)

Thus does one go to the stars; thus does one attain immortality.

(877)   sic transit gloria mundi (L.)

So passes away the glory of the world.

(878)   silent leges inter arma (L.)

The laws are silent in the midst of arms (i.e., in war-time).

(879)   similia similibus curantur (L.)

Like are cured by like; like diseases are cured by like remedies; a disease is cured by a medicine which if given to a normal person would induce the disease;—the doctrine of homeopathy.

(880)   sine nomine vulgus (L.)

The common people without a name; the nameless multitude; the indescribable throng; the unworthy herd.

(881)   sine odio (L.)

Without hatred; without animosity; without ill will; without malice.

(882)   sine praejudicio (L.)

Without prejudice; without bias; without partiality.

(883)   sine qua non (L.)

Without which not; an essential quality; something absolutely necessary; that which is indispensable; a vital prerequisite.

(884)   sol lucet omnibus (L.)

The sun shines for all.

(885)   sola nobilitas virtus (L.)

Virtue is the only (true) nobility.

(886)   solamen curarum (L.)

A comfort of (from) cares; a refuge from anxieties.

(887)   soles qui nobis pereunt et imputantur (L.)

Days that pass and are reckoned against us.

(888)   spectemur agendo (L.)

Let us be judged by our deeds (or actions).

(889)   speculum vitae (L.)

The mirror of life; the reflection of life.

(890)   sperate miseri, cavete felices (L.)

Hope, you (who are) wretched—beware, you (who are) happy.

(891)   spero meliora (L.)

I hope for better things; I hope for better days.

(892)   spes sibi quisque (L.)

Let each person be his own hope; each person must rely upon himself; each man must pin his hopes upon himself.

(893)   splendide mendax (L.)

Splendidly mendacious; admirably deceptive.

(894)   stans pede in uno (L.)

Standing on one foot;—often used to designate a precarious foothold or position, or a period of short duration (as long as one can stand on one foot).

(895)   stare super vias antiquas (L.)

To stand upon the old ways; to remain faithful to the ancient ways; to remain conservative.

(896)   stat magni nominis umbra (L.)

The shadow of a great name stands (remains).

(897)   status quo (L.)

The state in which; the state in which an affair is or was at a specified time; the existing condition.

(898)   status quo ante (L.)

The state of affairs as it existed before; the former state or condition; the situation as it existed before a specified event or time.

(899)   stilus virum arguit (L.)

The style proves the man; the manner of doing reveals the man.

(900)   studiis et rebus honestis (L.)

For studies and honorable achievements.

(901)   studium immane loquendi (L.)

A fierce zeal for talking; a monumental fondness for talking.

(902)   sua cuique sunt vitia (L.)

Everyone has his own vices; each person has his own kind of faults.

(903)   sua cique voluptas (L.)

Everyone enjoys his own form of pleasure.

(904)   sua si bona norint (L.)

If only they knew their own blessings; if only they appreciated their good fortune.

(905)   suaviter in modo, fortiter in re (L.)

Agreeable in manner, firm in deed; gentle in manner, firm in action; with a velvet glove but an iron hand; with gentleness but firmness.

(906)   subpoena ad testificandum (L.)

A writ commanding a person to appear in court and testify as a witness.

(907)   subpoena duces tecum (L.)

A writ commanding a person to appear in court and bring with him certain specified documents.

(908)   sufficit (L.)

It suffices; it is enough; it will do.

(909)   summa cum laude (L.)

With the highest praise;—an inscription used in diplomas.

(910)   summum jus, summa injuria (L.)

The highest law, the greatest injustice; the stricter the law, the more severe the possible injury; rigorous enforcement of the law may result in painful injustice.

(911)   suppressio veri (L.)

Suppression of the truth.

(912)   suppressio veri, suggestio falsi (L.)

Suppression of the truth (is) the suggestion of a falsehood; suppressing what is true amounts to suggesting that which is false.

(913)   suum cuique tribuere (L.)

To give to each his own; to grant to each person his due.

(914) tacent: satis laudant (L.)

They are silent—they praise enough; their silence is praise enough;—said esp. of virulent critics.

(915) tâche sans tache (F.)

A job without a fault; a work without a blemish.

(916) tam facti quam animi (L.)

As much in deed as in intention; as much in act as in profession.

(917) tangere vulnus (L.)

To touch a wound; to touch a tender (sore) spot; to bring up a painful subject.

(918) tant il est vrai (F.)

So true is it; it is so true.

(919) Te Deum laudamus (L.)

We praise thee, God.

(920) tempora mutantur, nos et mutamur in illis (L.)

Times change, and we change in (with) them.

(921)   *tempori parendum (L.)*

One must yield to the (demands of the changing) times.

(922)   *tempus edax rerum (L.)*

Time (is) the devourer (destroyer) of things.

(923)   *tempus fugit (L.)*

Time flies; time passes swiftly; time has wings; life is short.

(924)   *tempus omnia revelat (L.)*

Time reveals everything; time explains everything; things become clear in time.

(925)   *testis unus, estis nullus (L.)*

One witness, no witness; one witness is regarded as no witness at all.

(926)   *tibi seris, tibi metis (L.)*

You sow for yourself, you reap for yourself; as you sow, so shall you reap.

(927)   *timeo hominem unius libri (L.)*

I fear the man of one book; I fear the man who knows one book (or subject), and knows it thoroughly.

(928)   *totis viribus (L.)*

With all of one's might; with all of one's power; with all of one's manliness.

(929)   *toto caelo errare (L.)*

To err by the whole extent of the heaven; to make a monumental mistake; to err grievously; to be greatly mistaken.

(930)   tour d'ivoire (F.)

An ivory tower; a place suitable for withdrawing from reality, as for contemplation; an attitude of aloofness; a position of delicate reserve.

(931)   tourner casaque (F.)

To turn one's coat; to desert one's party; to change sides; to abandon principles; to rat on one's friends.

(932)   tout bien ou rien (F.)

Everything well or not a thing; one should do the whole thing well, or not attempt it at all.

(933)   tout comprendre c'est tout pardonner (F.)

To understand all is to pardon all; to understand, often means to forgive.

(934)   tout est dit (F.)

All has been said; all has been spoken of; all has been covered.

(935)   tout est perdu fors l'honneur (F.)

All is lost but honor;—words attributed to Francis I following his defeat at Pavia.

(936)   tout le monde est sage après coup (F.)

The whole world (i.e., everyone) is wise after the event (has taken place); everyone is a prophet after something has happened.

(937)   tout vient à point à qui sait attendre (F.)

Everything comes properly to him who knows how to wait; everything comes to him who waits; patience brings all things eventually.

(938)   *traduttori, traditori (It.)*

Translators are deceivers; translators are traitors to
the original; translators are betrayers with regard to the
author's style.

(939)   *trahison des clercs (F.)*

A betrayal of the scholars (intellectuals).

(940)   *tras los años viene el juicio (Sp.)*

After the years comes the judgment; wisdom comes
with years.

(941)   *tu ne cede malis (L.)*

Do not yield to adversity; do not surrender to misfortune.

U

(942) *ubi jus, ibi remedium (L.)*

Where there is a right, there is a remedy; where there is a rightful claim, there is a way of asserting it.

(943) *ubi jus incertum, ibi jus nullum (L.)*

Where the law is uncertain, there is no law.

(944) *ubiquiste (F.)*

A person who seems to be, or tries to be, everywhere at the same time; a ubiquitous person.

(945) *Übung macht den Meister (G.)*

Practice makes the master; practice makes the craftsman; practice makes perfect.

(946) *un homme averti en vaut deux (F.)*

One man warned is worth two (men not warned) ; forewarned is forearmed.

(947) *un malheur amène son frère (F.)*

One misfortune introduces its brother; one misfortune leads to another.

(948) *un malheur ne vient jamais seul (F.)*

A misfortune never comes alone; one misfortune always brings another.

(949) *una scopa nuova spazza bene (It.)*
A new broom sweeps well (clean).

(950) *undank ist der Welt Lohn (G.)*
Ingratitude is the universal reward.

(951) *une fois n'est pas coutume (F.)*
(Doing something) one time is not a habit.

(952) *uni navi ne committas omnia (L.)*
Do not put all your goods in one ship; do not put all your eggs in one basket.

(953) *usque ad aras (L.)*
1. As far as the altars; all the way except in matters which are contrary to one's religion. 2. Even to and including the altars, i.e., to the finish, to the final sacrifice.

(954) *usque ad nauseam (L.)*
Even to nausea; to the point of disgust; so far as to cause repugnance.

(955) *usus est tyrannus (L.)*
Custom is a tyrant; established usage (social convention) is a cruel taskmaster.

(956) *usus te plura docebit (L.)*
Experience will teach you very many things.

(957) *uti, non abuti (L.)*
To use, not to abuse (or misuse).

V

(958)   vade retro me, Satana! (L.)

Get thee behind me, Satan!

(959)   vagissant (fem. vagissante) (F.)

Whimpering; whining; puling; crying; wailing.

(960)   valeat quantum valere potest (L.)

Let it pass for what it is worth; let it be taken for what it is worth.

(961)   vel caeco appareat (L.)

It would be obvious (apparent) even to a blind man.

(962)   veneum in auro bibitur (L.)

Poison is (often) drunk out of gold (cups); evil often comes out of good.

(963)   venienti occurrite morbo (L.)

Attack a disease as it comes;—i.e., before it gets a foothold.

(964)   verbatim, litteratim, et punctatim (L.)

Word for word, letter for letter, and point for point; precisely as recorded in the original.

(965)   *verbum sat sapienti (est) (L.)*

A word to the wise (is) enough; one word of caution to the wise is sufficient.

(966)   *veritas nihil veretur nisi abscondi (L.)*

Truth fears nothing except concealment (or suppression).

(967)   *veritas praevalebit (L.)*

Truth will prevail; truth will triumph in the end.

(968)   *veritas temporis filia (L.)*

Truth is the daughter of time; truth will out in time.

(969)   *veritatis simplex oratio est (L.)*

The language of truth is simple; the truth speaks in straighforward terms.

(970)   *via trita, via tuta (L.)*

The well-trodden way, the safe way; the beaten path is the safe path.

(971)   *vide et crede (L.)*

See and believe; see and be convinced.

(972)   *vide ut supra (L.)*

See what is given above; see what is stated above.

(973)   *video meliora proboque, deteriora sequor (L.)*

I see and approve the better things, (but) I follow the worse.

(974) vigilantibus, non dormientibus, jura subveniunt (L.)

The laws assist the vigilant, not the sleeping (i.e., not those who are apathetic or unconcerned).

(975) vincam aut moriar (L.)

I will conquer or I will die.

(976) vincit omnia veritas (L.)

The truth conquers all things; the truth prevails; the truth overcomes all obstacles.

(977) vincit qui patitur (L.)

He conquers who endures; he wins who bears patiently; he triumphs who perseveres.

(978) vincit qui se vincit (L.)

He conquers who conquers himself; he is a real conqueror who conquers himself; he conquers others who conquers himself first.

(979) virtus in actione consistit (L.)

Courage consists of (i.e., is expressed in) action.

(980) virtus in arduis (L.)

Courage (or steadfastness) in the midst of difficulties.

(981) virtus incendit vires (L.)

Courage kindles (arouses) strength.

(982) virtus laudatur, et alget (L.)

Virtue is praised, and (usually) starves.

(983)   *virtus sola nobilitat (L.)*

Virtue alone ennobles a man; only virtue dignifies a person.

(984)   *virtute non viris (L.)*

By quality not by (the number of) men; by worth not by force.

(985)   *virtute securus (L.)*

Secure through strength and integrity of character.

(986)   *vita sine litteris mors est (L.)*

Life without books is (like) death.

(987)   *vitia erunt, donec homines (L.)*

As long as men (live), there will be faults; as long as there are men, there will be human vices.

(988)   *vitiis nemo sine nascitur (L.)*

No one is born without vices (or faults).

(989)   *vitium scriptoris (L.)*

A writer's error; an author's mistake; a secretary's error; a clerical error.

(990)   *vive ut vivas (L.)*

Live that you may live; live a life that will endure.

(991)   *voilà comme je suis (F.)*

That is the way I am; you must accept me as I am.

(992)   *voluntas reputatur pro facto (L.)*

The intention is to be reckoned (taken) for the deed.

(993) *Vorsicht ist die Mutter der Weisheit (G.)*

Prudence is the mother of wisdom; foresight is the mother of knowledge; discretion is the better part of valor.

(994) *vous y perdrez vos pas (F.)*

You will lose (waste) your steps there; you will waste your time.

(995) *vox audita perit, litera scripta manet (L.)*

The word that is heard perishes, (but) the written letter remains.

(996) *vox, et praeterea nihil (L.)*

A voice, and beyond this nothing; a voice and nothing more; a senseless sound.

(997)   wer A sagt muss auch B sagen (G.)

Whosoever says A must also say B; he who begins something must also finish it.

(998)   wer nie sein Brot mit Thränen ass! (G.)

Who is the man who never his bread with tears (sorrow) ate!

(999)   wer wagt gewinnt (G.)

Who dares wins; he who ventures gains.

(1000) Zeitgeist (G.)

The spirit of the time; the spirit of the age; the pulse
or trend of a given period.

Part II

Index to Elegant Phrases

Explanatory Note on the Index

THE FOLLOWING INDEX was prepared in order to enable the user of the book to find a suitable elegant phrase with which to express, accentuate, or embellish a particular concept or thought. For this purpose, the *meanings* of the elegant phrases were arranged in alphabetical order for this index. In some cases the meanings were slightly modified, to make them more useful for the purpose of the index. In a few cases, the word order was changed, in order to put the most significant word first. For example, the meaning "to the utmost of one's ability" was entered under "Ability," so that the meaning or concept reads "Ability, to the utmost of one's." Where it was felt necessary, an idea or meaning was entered in two ways, in each case starting with a different word. This makes the finding of the meaning or thought easier.

Each thought or meaning in the Index is followed by a number. The number refers to the first part of the book, where the Elegant Phrases are listed numerically as well as alphabetically. For example, if the user of the book wants an elegant expression for an idea involving absurdity, and specifically for the idea "Reduction to absurdity," he would look under "Reduction" or under "Absurdity." In both instances, under "Reduction to absurdity" and under "Absurdity, reduction to," the number following the entry in the Index is 825. Referring to the first part of the book, the number 825 gives the reader the elegant phrase "Reductio ad absurdum." By spending a few minutes with the book, the reader will convince himself that the finding of an appropriate elegant phrase is a simple matter.

A

Abandon principles; change sides; turn one's coat — 931
A word to the intelligent is sufficient — 568
Ability, in a condition of having the — 555
Ability, to the utmost of one's — 69
Abode of fools; folls' paradise — 604
About the time or year stated — 246
Above all others; in the highest degree of excellence — 745
Above-mentioned place, in the — 612
Above: see what is given above; see the preceding — 972
Absence, in the; during the absence (of the person involved) — 530
Abstract, in the; regarded apart from any particular case — 531
Absurd; — said of an argument or reasoning — 47
Absurdity, method of showing — 825
Absurdity, reduction to — 825
Abundance of caution does not hurt — 60
Abuse does not militate against proper use — 62
Abuse is no argument against sensible use — 401
Abuse: to use, not to abuse — 957
Accepted, it is — 229
Accepted piece of nonsense; convenient myth — 427
Accepted standards of words — 786
Accident, because or through an — 402
Accidentally, through an accident — 402
Acclaim; applause; demonstration of approval — 355
Accolade: let him who deserves it get the accolade — 744
Accomplished fact; something that has already been done — 432
Accomplished labors are pleasant — 580
Accord, in; in harmony; in agreement — 373

131

According to accepted custom — 860
According to good practices — 860
According to regular procedure — 309
According to the case that has arisen — 414
According to the rule — 309
According to the value—87
According to what is equitable and right—859
Account, on; in part payment—15
Achievement: through difficulties to the highest achievement—755
Achievements: for studies and honorable achievements —900
Acquainted with the matter at hand—148
Act: as much in act as in profession—916
Act: by the act itself; by the mere act or fact—572
Act foolishly at times—323
Action: courage is expressed in action—979
Action: gentle in manner, firm in action—905
Action, military, French award for bravery in—282
Action, not words—429
Action, policy of; new line of action—319
Action speaks louder than words—430
Action, while in the heat of—347
Actions: let us be judged by our actions—888
Acts are proven or vindicated by the result—422
Admiration: to admire nothing; to wonder at nothing— 693
Admission to a society, association, etc.—195
Admitting to the same rank or degree, as in a university —68
Adorn: he adorned everything that he touched—692
Adventurous businessman—380
Adversities: after so many adversities, finally good luck —767
Adversities: through adversities to the stars—755
Adversity, do not yield to—941
Adversity: through adversity to the pinnacle—754
Advice: better advice comes after a night's sleep—189
Affairs, not qualified mentally to handle one's—703
Affected style, without—847
After darkness comes light—766
After death of the patient, the doctor; too late—134

After midday; after noon—764
After so many adversities, finally good luck—767
After so many shipwrecks, finally the harbor—760
After the event: everyone is wise after the event—936
After the stroke; too late—133
After the years comes the judgment—940
Against good manners—263
Against the evil of death there is no medicine in the garden—264
Against the grain—36
Against the world—265
Age, old: youthful or vigorous old age—283
Age: spirit of the age—1000
Ages and ages, for; forever and ever—556
Agreeable change of circumstances—579
Agreeable in manner, firm in deed—905
Agreeable madness—104
Agreed, it is—229
Agreed-upon fable; convenient myth—427
Agreement, in; in sympathetic relationship—373
Agreements should be honored—743
Aid: not for such aid or for such defenders does this situation call—715
Alas, the fleeting years glide by—362
Alienated from himself; insane—100
All good with you! To your health!—185
All goods in one ship, do not put—952
All has been said; everything has been covered—934
All hope is not gone yet—717
All is lost but honor—935
All learn from one—55
All: not for oneself but for all—713
All over again; anew—29
All over; entirely; from head to heel—9
All that glitters is not gold—697
All the way except matters which are contrary to one's religion—953
All things are for the glory of God—734
All things change (in time)—735
All together; as a unit—560
All together; counting all; in all—375
All together; in a mass—369

Aloud; in loud tones—21

Altars: as far as and including the altars; to the finish —953

Altars: as far as the altars; as far as one's religion permits—953

Alternately; in shifts—102

Always faithful—862

Always; forever; in eternity—534

Always; from eternity till the present—48

Always: now and always; now and forever—738

Ambiguity, in; in doubt; in obscurity—535

Ambitions, set a limit to your—228

Amends, honorable—110

Ancient ways: remain faithful to the ancient ways—895

And all of this kind—391

And all this sort of thing—391

And even when a wound is healed the scar remains—397

And he grows worse with treatment—91

And once uttered, a word flies irrevocably away—392

And others—389

And others of similar kind—390

And so on; and so forth—390

And the following—393

And the rest or remaining—390

And you too, Brutus!—394

Anesthesia, partial; twilight sleep—297

Anew; from a fresh beginning—53

Anew; from the beginning; all over again—29

Anger: greatest remedy for anger is a delay—631

Angry: him whom God wishes to destroy he first makes angry—798

Angry: those whom Jupiter wishes to destroy he first makes mad or angry—819

Animal, in the living;—as opposed to an experimental environment—563

Animal that is man; species of animal that is man—479

Animation, with; with spirit—160

Animosity: without animosity; without hatred—881

Annually; yearly; for each year—753

Answer, if you please—828

Answer: request for an answer to an invitation—828

Antidote: do not take the antidote before the poison—
675
Antiquity, from; of yore—50
Anxieties, refuge from—886
Anxiety: dismiss this anxiety from your breast—651
Anxiety: my anxiety is for the future—646
Apology, humble, to an offended person—110
Apostate from Judaism—645
Apparent: it would be apparent even to a blind man—
961
Appearance: judge a tree by its fruit, not by its leaves—
470
Appearance, on the first—778
Appearance, there is no relying on—469
Appearances, do not rely on—674
Appetite, something served to whet the—130
Appetizer served at the beginning of a meal—515
Appetizer served before a meal;—*Italian*—130
Applause; acclaim; demonstration of approval—355
Appraisal, without critical; without discrimination; with
open mouth, in the manner of a hungry young bird—7
Approval, demonstration of; acclaim; applause—355
Approval, official, of a published work—528
Approve: I see and approve the better things but I
follow the worse—973
Approximate date, word indicating—246
Arbitrary; arrogant; highhanded—502
Ardent wish; passionate desire—322
Ardent words; heated words—139
Ardently; with warmth—160
Ardor; dash; vigor—364
Ardor divinely inspired; sacred fire—445
Arduous circumstances, level head in—642
Argument based on what has already been conceded—
143
Argument: before the argument began—128
Argument collapses; question falls down—216
Argument, death is the last—662
Argument directed to good sense—141
Argument directed to reasoning or judgment—141
Argument directed to sympathy, pity, etc.—142

At a good price; at a bargain price—6
At all cost; at any price—43
At any risk; at any price—42
At first sight—33
At great expense or sacrifice—20
At length; in a prolix manner—82
At long last; finally—22
At my own risk—644
At once; forthwith; here and now—505
At pleasure; as much as one wishes—80
At pleasure of the performer; at the tempo chosen by the
    performer;—esp. in music—11
At the crossroads—65
At the house of—243
At your pleasure; by your permission—187
Attack a disease as it comes—963
Attack: under attack from both sides—378
Attempt something hazardous—250
Attempt: this attempt ended in failure—506
Attempt to do the impossible—775
Attitude of aloofness; ivory tower—930
Attitude of indifference—693
Attractiveness, tormenting—169
Auspicious words, let us speak—326
Author; man of the pen—510
Author, name assumed by an; pen name—701
Author, principal work of an—239
Author, uncontrollable urge to be an—215
Author, unknown or little known—151
Author who writes for selected readers—856
Author who writes for the elite—856
Author whose work is not fully appreciated—151
Authoritative sources, draw knowledge from—566
Authority, paper giving one full—223
Author's mistake; writer's error—989
Authors; writers; men of letters—476
Authors; writers; persons of the pen—478
Avidly; hungrily; with open mouth, in the manner of a
    hungry young bird—7
Award for bravery, French—282
Awkward; clumsy; left-handed—475

B

Babes: out of the mouth of babes comes the truth—412
Bachelor of arts—145
Back, from the; from the rear—38
Back side of a leaf, as of a book—466
Bad luck . . . See also under **Misfortune.** 948, 673, 941, 947
Bad to worse, from—305
Balance, in; in harmony; in equilibrium—533
Ballad, rendered in the style of a—1
Ballet dancer, female professional—302
Ballet dancer, male professional—301
Baptism of fire—163
Bargain, at a good; at a good price; cheap—6
Base cause, person perversely upholding a—90
Based on experience—32
Basis of comparison—788
Bastard; son of nobody known—458
Be greatly mistaken; err by the whole extent of the heaven—929
Be present ye faithful—89
Be what you appear to be; be yourself—388
Bear, and you shall be borne with—442
Bearing, fine; fine air—171
Beautiful arts; fine arts—170
Beautiful disorder—166
Beautiful gesture; noble act—167
Beautiful letters; fine literature—178
Beautiful song—172
Beautiful spirit—173
Beautiful world; elegant world—168
Beauty of the devil—169
Beauty which bewitches—169
Before Christ—127
Before the litigation began—128
Before . . . See also under subject, as **Noon.** 129
Begin: do not begin unless you mean to finish—678
Begin: whoever begins something must also finish it—997
Beginning, from a fresh; anew—53

Beginning, from the; anew; all over again—29
Beginning, from the; from the origin of the thing—54
Beginning, from the very; at first sight—33
Beginning: he has half finished who has begun—328
Beginning, to the; at the beginning—76
Beguile: world likes to be beguiled—669
Begun is half done—328
Behind, from; from the rear—38
Behold the end of our labors!—462
Behold the man!—354
Being alive: living is not merely being alive but being well—706
Belated reward—245
Believe: see and believe; see and be convinced—971
Believe: understand so that you may believe—567
Beloved; dear; darling—242
Benefit cannot be bestowed on one who is not willing—186
Benefit: For whose benefit?—287
Benefit: he who enjoys the benefit of a thing should also feel the burden—808
Benefit: small benefit from much effort—351
Best of the best—277
Betrayal of the scholars—939
Better advice comes after the night—189
Better late than never;—*Italian*—636
Better things: I hope for better things—891
Better things: I see and approve the better things but I follow the worse—973
Better things, let us turn to—83
Between the leaves is the fruit—569
Between two fires; under two assaults—378
Between us; between ourselves; confidentially—379
Beware: hope you who are wretched, beware you who are happy—890
Beware thou of him; beware of that man—518
Bewitching beauty—169
Beyond comparison; in the highest degree of excellence—745
Bias: without bias; without partiality; without prejudice—882
Big head, little sense—492

Billowy; bulging; puffed—210
Bird: early bird catches the worm—659
Bird; to each bird its own nest is beautiful—12
Bird, young, like a; with open mouth; avidly—7
Birds of a feather; persons of the same dough—477
Birth: he is well born, well dressed, and only moderately
    well learned—183
Birth, of the same—363
Bitter, something; something unpleasant—106
Blameable, not; not guilty—704
Blemish: work without a blemish—915
Blessed memory, of—165
Blessings: if only they knew their own blessings—904
Blessings: it would be good if they appreciated their
    blessings—206
Blind man: it would be obvious even to a blind man—961
Bloom of youth—169
Blow for blow; for a good deed a good return—3
Blow; stroke; maneuver—273
Blue ribbon; high distinction—268
Bluestocking; learned woman; literary woman—441
Blunder in social manners; a false step—437
Boastful statement, prefatory remark for a—58
Body and mind, sound in—844
Body and mind, vigor of—839
Body: examination of a human body after death—765
Body of law; collection of all laws of a country—270
Body of laws created by legislation or enactment—589
Body of the crime or offense—269
Body of the victim in a case of murder—269
Body: sound mind in a healthy body—643
Bones: for those who come late, nothing but the bones—
    865
Bones: may his bones rest in peace—653
Book censor; book critic—227
Book: I fear the man of one book—927
Book knowledge, learned with—331
Book, left-hand page of a—466
Book, license to print or publish a—528
Book, right-hand page of a—465
Books, avid reader of; bookworm—503
Books: from the books of—408
Books, glutton for; bookworm—503

Books have their own peculiar fortunes—496
Books: life without books is like death—986
Books: years teach more than books—575
Bookworm; avid reader; glutton for books—503
Bored; tired; weary—377
Born: no one is born without vices—988
Boy: do not entrust a boy with a dangerous weapon—676
Boy: do not give a man's job to a boy—676
Boy: do not give a sword to a boy—676
Boy who has reached his thirteenth year and has thus
    become responsible for the observance of the religious
    law;—in Hebrew religion—164
Brave man; heart of a lion—251
Bravery in action, French award for—282
Bravo! Well done! Continue in your excellent way—616
Bread: Who is the man who never his bread with tears
    ate—998
Break: you may break me, but you shall not bend me—
    468
Brevity is the root of speech—591
Brevity is the soul of wit—591
Bribe; gratuity; gift—340
Bride: neither by prayer nor by bribe—680
Brilliance, display of; splendor; acclaim—355
Brilliant maneuver—273
Bronze: monument more lasting than bronze—657
Broom: new broom sweeps clean—949
Brusquely; point-blank; to one's face—8
Brutus, and you too—394
Bulging; protuberant; puffed—210
Bunch of hirelings; band of mercenaries—491
Burden: he who feels the benefit of a thing should also
    feel the burden—808
Burden: nothing burdens so heavily as a secret—836
Burning words; ardent words—139
Burst; explosion; display of brilliance—355
Burst of enthusiasm; ardor; vigor—364
Business owners: policy of the government which allows
    business owners to set their own rules of competition
    —594-595
Business: person who is fond of undertaking a risky but
    promising business—380
Businessman, adventurous; enterprising person—380

By badly narrating a story is spoiled—627
By courage, not by craft—121
By equity; by justice; in fairness—304
By faith, not by arms—453
By grace; by favor—306
By itself; in itself; as such; inherently—756
By quality, not by quantity—763
By quality not by the number of men—984
By reason of something done after a particular event—413
By teaching we learn—330
By the fact itself; by the mere fact—572
By the gift or grace of God—406
By the way; in passing; incidentally—371
By the year; for each year—753
By this title; under this name—508
By weight, not by number—763
By what means, who, what, where, etc.—815
By word of mouth; orally—46
By worth not by force—984
Byways of wisdom—861

C

Caesar: render unto Caesar the things that are Caesar's—824
Caesar, saying attributed to;—on his crossing the Rubicon—574
Caesar's words to Brutus—394
Calendar, reflection on the—887
Calm in raging waves—843
Calm mind, preserve a—94
Calmness of mind, with—95, 96
Candor, with; with sincerity; from the open heart—14
Canon law; law governing religious affairs of a Christian church—585
Canons of the Roman Catholic Church—271
Capital judgment; sentence of death—581
Capitalists; wealthy class;—as opposed to the working class—211
Caprice; prank; whim—222

Card, blank; full authority—223
Care: dismiss this care from your heart—651
Care: freedom from care; freedom from worry—847
Care: I do not have, desire, or care—679
Care, in your; into thy hands—547
Care: without care; without worry; without anxiety—849
Carefree; gay; without worry—849
Careful, one cannot be too—60
Careless: do a job in a careless manner—842
Cares, comfort from—886
Case: according to the case that has arisen—414
Case, for this; for this case only—72
Case is closed; question falls down—216
Case of sheer necessity—224
Cause, righteous or just—590
Cause to effect, from; from a generalization to a particular case—34
Caution does not hurt, even when in abundance—60
Caution: trust, but be careful whom you trust—454
Celebration; festival; feast—*Spanish*—457
Celebration; festival; festive occasion—444
Celebration marking the admission of a person to the membership of a society—195
Censor of books—227
Certainly; yes indeed—573
Chaff: from much chaff a little grain—351
Change: all things change (with the years)—735
Change: one must yield to the demands of the changing times—921
Change sides; desert one's party; turn one's coat—931
Change the name and the story fits you—310
Change the subject, let us; let us turn to better things—83
Change: time is the greatest changer of things—632
Change: times change and we change with them—920
Chapel style, in; without instrumental accompaniment—10
Charity begins at home—777
Charity begins with oneself—777
Charming faults, they abound with or in—61
Cheap; at a good price; at a bargain price—6

Cherished one; dear; well beloved—190
Cherished one; sweetheart—242
Child; to a mother her own child is always beautiful—12
Childhoood, from; from the tender years—37
Childhood, from one's; from the cradle—52
Choice, free; free will—602
Choice selection, as of literary passages—823
Choral singing in chapel style, without instrumental ac-
    companiment—10
Christ, before—127
Christ: for Christ and the church—244
Christ, in the year before—122
Christ, in the year of—123
Christ, representation of, as a lamb—97
Church: for Christ and the church—244
Church, law governing the religious affairs of a—585
Circle of the sciences—739
Circumlocution, by; in a roundabout way—751
Circumlocution, without; without affectation in style—
    847
Circumstances, agreeable change of—579
Circumstances, in accordance with the—414
Citation: in the first place cited—611
Citation: in the place cited—610
Citation: in the place cited above—612
Citation: which see; which look up—818
Civil law; law dealing with private rights—586
Claim: where there is a rightful claim, there is a way of
    asserting it—942
Clarification: things become clear in time; time reveals
    everything—924
Classes of society in easy circumstances—249
Classical writer; author who writes for the elite—856
Clerical error; secretary's error—990
Clever act; sudden and successful move—273
Clever person; beautiful spirit—173
Cleverness, sprightly; sparkling intelligence—385
Clothes do not make the man—286
Clumsy; awkward; left-handed—475
Coat: turn one's coat; desert one's party—931
Cobbler, stick to your last—854
Coffee, black—220

Coffee, black, the color of—220
Coffee with milk—219
Coffee with milk, the color of—219
Collection, choice;—as of literary passages—823
Collection of laws, as of a given country—270
College, within the walls of a—570
Come in; enter;—an invitatioon or an order—381
Come to naught after a long series of successes—672
Come to ruin at the very beginning—672
Comfort from cares—886
Comfort; restfulness; well-being—191
Command: the more gently one commands, the better he
    is complied with—650
Commentators, with notes by many—295
Common law; unwritten law—600
Common people without a name; nameless multitude—
    880
Common sense, to; to good judgment—78
Comparison, basis for—788
Comparison, beyond; in the highest degree of excellence
    —745
Comparison: if it is permitted to compare small things
    with great—873
Compassion: God have compassion for us—324
Completion crowns the work—461
Compliance: the more gently one commands, the better
    he is complied with—650
Composed in face of turmoil—843
Composure, with—95, 96
Concealment: truth fears nothing except concealment—
    966
Conceived, well; well invented—180
Conclusion, logic of coming to a—822
Concord: victory is always there where concord is—520
Condemnation, expression of. Down with!—2
Condemnation: they condemn that which they do not
    understand—298
Condition as it existed before—898
Condition: existing condition; state in which something
    is—897
Conduct, judge in matters of—137
Confidence: he who lost confidence lost everything—456

Cross purposes, at—41
Crossroads, at the—65
Crucial experiment; critical test—423
Crude; clumsy; left-handed—475
Crying; wailing; puling—959
Cupidity; love of money—112
Cups: poison is often drunk out of gold cups—962
Currency . . . See also under **Money.**—71
Custom: according to accepted custom—860
Custom demanding sexual abstinence of a married couple
    on their wedding night—343
Custom is a tyrant—955
Customs: things that were once vices are now customs—
    791

Damned soul—107
Dance of death—300
Dancer, female, esp. a professional—302
Dancer, male, esp. a professional—301
Dancing procession of skeletons—300
Danger, first exposure to extreme—163
Danger in delay, there is—758
Danger, unsuspected—116
Dare: he who dares wins—999
Dare to be discreet; dare to be prudent—850
Dare to be wise—152
Dare to be wise; dare to be sensible—850
Dare to do the right thing—152
Daring: first weigh, then dare—384
Darkness: after darkness comes light—766
Darling; dear; beloved—242
Dash; vigor; ardor—364
Date regarded as approximate, word designating—246
Daughter: truth is the daughter of time—593
Day, from that; from then on—17
Day of festivity; holiday—457
Day of rest from regular work; holiday—*Spanish*—457
Day to day, to live from—540
Days: I hope for better days—891

Destitute, the; outcasts; unfortunate ones—599
Destroyer of things, time is the—922
Determine the facts—793
Devil, beauty of the—169
Devil's advocate—90
Devotion of the members of a group to the group as a whole—386
Devourer of things, time is the—922
Die: I will conquer or I will die—975
Die is cast; decision is made—519
Die is cast; it is all decided—99
Die is cast;—saying attributed to Caesar—574
Die, not all of me shall—708
Die . . . See also under **Death.**—425, 765, 264, 274, 314, 455, 245, 874, 633, 661, 662, 986, 768, 660, 581, 25, 312
Difficult circumstances, remember to preserve a calm mind in—94
Difficult situation, level head in a—642
Difficulties: death resolves all difficulties—660
Difficulties: through difficulties to splendor—752
Difficulties: through difficulties to the highest achievement—755
Difficulties: through difficulties to the stars—754
Difficulty: example which resolves one difficulty by introducing another accomplishes nothing—694
Difficulty: faced with two equally harassing situations—378
Difficulty: settle one difficulty by creating another—606
Difficulty worthy of its resolver—327
Difficulty . . . See also under **Misfortune.**—948, 673, 941, 947
Dignify: virtue alone dignifies a person—983
Digression: let us return to the subject—835
Diligence, quiet; leisurely assiduity—741
Diligence, with; with perseverance—259
Diploma: with praise—293
Diplomas, tribute used in: with great praise or honor—617
Diplomas, tribute used in: with praise or honor—293
Disabled; out of action—49
Disappointment, grave; sorrow; heartbreak—278

Disapproval, expression of. Down with!—2

Discourse is the index of the mind—864

Discovery: exclamation of joy on discovering something —399

Discreet: dare to be discreet; dare to be prudent—850

Discretion is the better part of valor—993

Discretion, seasoned; mature wisdom—649

Discrimination, without; at random—41

Discrimination, without; with open mouth, in the manner of a hungry young bird—7

Disease for which physicians have no remedy—737

Disease: treatment is worse than the disease—91

Disease without an organic basis—592

Disease without disease—592

Diseases: critical diseases call for drastic remedies—159

Disgrace of physicians—737

Disgust: to the point of disgust; even to nausea—954

Disgust: to the point of disgust; to nausea—85

Disgusting extreme, to a—85

Dish, main, of a meal—761

Dish served at the beginning of a meal, as an appetizer —515

Dishonor: rather to die than to be dishonored—768

Dismiss this anxiety from your breast—651

Disorder, beautiful; pleasing confusion—166

Display of brilliance; splendor; acclaim—355

Display one's wit—771

Disproving, method of—825

Dispute begets dispute—605

Dispute by dispute, example which settles—694

Dispute: resolve dispute with dispute—606

Disputes; new disputes on old accounts—45

Disqualified; out of action—49

Dissention: no one dissenting; unanimously—683

Distinction, high; blue ribbon—268

Distinction, with the greatest—630

Distinguish: he who distinguishes well teaches well—801

Distinguished person, in emulation of a—826

Ditty; comic song; short song—234

Diversion: something that diverts attention from the facts—769

Divide and rule—329

E

Each person must rely upon himself—892
Each: to each one his own kind—288
Eagerness divinely inspired; sacred fire—445
Eagerness for action; dash; ardor—364
Eagle does not catch flies—135
Earliest recollections, from one's; from the cradle—52
Early bird catches the worm—659
Early hours are auspicious ones—659
Early to bed and early to rise makes a man healthy,
  wealthy, and wise—659
Early years, from the; from childhood—37
Ears, ass is recognized by his—404
Earth: let justice be done though the earth crashes—450
Earth: much on this earth, little in heaven—665
Easy come, easy go—776
Easy does it; step by step one goes quite far—747
Edition, first, a copy of a—361
Edition, first, as of a book—361
Education: he is well born, well dressed, and only
  moderately well learned—183
Education, man having a high—511
Effort, make every; move every stone—733
Effort: small benefit from much effort—351
Either do not start, or else finish—158
Elder; senior member; dean—341
Elegant collection, as of literary passages—823
Elixir of life—365
Eloquence: enough of eloquence but too little of wisdom
  —852
Emergency, for an; for any occasion that may arise—783
Emotion, with; with love—257
Emphasis, without; in passing—371
Empire of letters; domain of literature—366
Empirical; based on experience—32
Employee: let the employer answer (for his employee)
  —834
Employer: let the employer answer (for his employee)
  —834
Empty dreams—93

Emulation of a distinguished person, in—826
Encourage the others, to—770
End, consider the; be mindful of the outcome—459
End crowns the work—461
End: it is the end; it is all over—460
End justifies the means—422
End, look to the; consider the possible outcome—833
End of labors, behold the—462
End of our labors is in sight—462
End of the world—483
End, perceive the; consider the outcome—161
End, to the very; at the end—70
Endless desire for praise—596
Endlessly; to infinity—75
Endlessness of time and/or space, in the—546
Endurance: he conquers who endures—977
Enemy pretending to be a friend—116
Enjoyment of life, keen—578
Enlightenment, the Lord is my—336
Enmity among theologians—732
Enmity . . . See also under **Hatred.**—731, 732, 57, 881
Enough and beyond; enough and more than enough—853
Enough: it is enough; it will do; it suffices—908
Enough of eloquence but too little of wisdom—852
Enterprising person; adventurous businessman—380
Enthusiasm, burst of; dash; vigor—364
Entirely; all over; from head to heel—9
Entreaty: neither by entreaty nor by bribe—680
Entrust the rest to the gods—759
Envy: he who envies is an inferior person—804
Envy is blind—217
Envy, let there be no—57
Epic; poetry; poem—233
Epistolary war; a war of the pen—494
Equals, before one's—267
Equals, first among his—780
Equals . . . See also under **Peers.**—267, 780
Equanimity, with—95, 96
Equilibrium, in; in balance; in harmony—533
Equitable: according to what is equitable and right—859
Equity, by; by justice; in fairness—304
Err by the whole extent of the heaven—929

Err grieviously; make a monumental mistake—929
Err: to err is human—383, 517
Error, acknowledgment of one's—110
Error: clerical error; secretary's error—989
Error: writer's error; author's mistake—989
Errors: list of errors with their corrections—272
Essential quality; without which not (or nothing)—883
Establishment: let it be established—447
Eternally; everlastingly—534
Eternity, for; for life eternal—88
Eternity, for; in perpetuity—553
Eternity, from, till the present; always—48
Etiquette, error on a point of—437
Euphoria; well-being; comfort—191
Evasion, with—in a roundabout way—751
Even an oak is felled by many blows—668
Even including the altars; to the finish—953
Even one hair has its shadow—396
Even to nausea—954
Event, principal, in a series of events—761
Events, pleasant change in the course of—579
Events worth remembering; notable events—640
Eventualities, ready for all—552
Ever upward; higher;—a motto—418
Everybody learns from somebody; all learn from one—
    55
Everybody's secret; an open secret—858
Everyone enjoys his own form of pleasure—903
Everyone has his own vices—902
Everyone is wise after the event—936
Everyone knows the rest—232
Everyone must die; death is common to all—661
Everything comes properly to him who knows how to
    wait—937
Everything well or not a thing; do everything well or do
    not do at all—932
Everywhere: person who tries to be everywhere at the
    same time—944
Evil: he who speaks evil hears even worse—812
Evil-minded person—108
Evil often comes out of good—962
Evil, speaking, there is art even in—387
Evils, least of—648

Evils: of several evils choose the least—648
Exacting; fastidious; hard to please—421
Examination of a human body after death—765
Example of the king, in the—826
Example: we live more by example than by reason—420
Example which settles dispute by dispute accomplishes nothing—694
Excellence, in the highest degree of—745
Excellent! Splendid! Extremely well done—212
Excellent; splendid; magnificent;—*French*—623
Excellent; splendid; magnificent;—*Spanish*—622
Exception: no rule without an exception; every rule has an exception—726
Exception proves the rule—419
Excess: nothing to excess—677
Excitement, composed in face of—843
Exclamation of triumph on discovering something—399
Excuse admits existence of guilt—809
Exercise piece in music; practice piece—398
Existing condition; state in which something is—897
Exit; outlet, as for emotions—315
Expense, at great—20
Experience, based on—32
Experience: fools learn only from experience—400
Experience teaches more than books—574
Experience will teach you many things—956
Experiment, crucial; decisive test—423
Experiment: let the experiment be made on a worthless body—448
Expert; acquainted with the facts—148
Expert, as in art; connoisseur—254
Expert in the law—584
Explanation of something obscure in terms that are even more obscure—730
Exploits; deeds; things done—831
Expressed, well; well conceived—180
Exquisite, an; fastidious person—136
Extemporaneous; without preparation—415
Extended form, in; at length; in full—544
External quality, do not trust the—674
Eyes, dust in the—769
Eyes, wool over the—769

Fable agreed upon for convenience; convenient fable to
    explain something bothersome—428
Face: on the face of it—778
Face, to one's; point-blank; candidly; brusquely—8
Faced with two equally harassing situations—378
Fact: by the fact itself; by the mere fact—572
Fact, in; in truth; to be frank—376
Facts; deeds; things done—831
Facts, determine the—793
Facts proving the crime or offense—269
Facts: something that diverts attention from the facts
    —769
Facts which constitute the crime charged—269
Facts which form the environment of a legal case—831
Fail even before one gets a good start—672
Fail while on the verge of success—672
Fair and good, in accordance with what is—403
Fairness, in; by equity—304
Faith and courage, with—120
Faith: by faith, not by arms—453
Faith: he who loses faith has nothing more to lose—456
Faith: I will keep faith; I will observe the faith—867
Faith, strong and courageous through—407
Faith, upon my—614
Faithful: always faithful—862
Faithful: mindful and faithful—638
Faithful to the urn of ashes—455
Faithful unto death—455
Fall behind: he who does not move forward falls behind
    —805
False in one matter, false in all—434
False step; blunder in social manners—437
Fame: may his fame live forever—436
Familiarity breeds contempt—253
Farewell! Take good care!—184
Farewell; till we see each other again;—*Spanish*—499
Fashionable gathering—175
Fashionable society; high society—168
Fast life: person who lives a fast life—203

Fastidious; exacting; hard to please—421
Fatally; to the death—25
Fate is in our own hands; every person is the master of his own fate—426
Fate is sealed; die is cast—99
Fate, leave the rest to—759
Fate: let fate decide—303
Fate, with a kindly; with good luck—188
Fates guide the willing man, the unwilling they drag along—346
Fates of men, so go the—875
Fates: whither the Fates beckon—816
Father: as is the father so is the son—794
Fault: job without a fault—915
Fault, minor; minor transgression—289
Fault, uncontrollable urge to find—213
Faults: as long as men live there will be faults—987
Faults: everyone has his own faults—902
Faults: no one is born without faults—988
Favor, by; by grace—306
Favor, by mere;—rather than by obligation—409
Favor, in bad; in bad odor—370
Favor: one favor sires another favor—488
Fear: courage without fear—276
Fear was the first creator of gods in the world—779
Fear: without fear and without reproach—846
Feature, conspicuous; salient point—789
Feature, main; main dish—761
Feeling of loss—322
Feeling, out of the depths of—307
Fellowship; group spirit; togetherness—386
Female dancer, esp. a professional—302
Female professional singer—221
Fence, on the, with regard to an issue; with a leg on either side—13
Festival; celebration; festive occasion—444
Festival; feast; celebration—*Spanish*—457
Few words are sufficient for the intelligent—568
Fiction accepted by common consent to explain something bothersome—427
Fie! Shame on you!—446
Fight to the bitter end—493

Fighting name; battle name; war name—700
Finally; at last—22
Find out, we shall; we shall see—722
Fine air; fine bearing—171
Fine arts school—358
Fine view; fair outlook—177
Finish: do not start unless you mean to finish—678
Finish: to the finish; to the altars—953
Finish: whoever begins must finish—997
Finished: it is finished; it is done—262, 431
Finishing stroke or blow—274
Fire, baptism of—163
Fire comes from fire—51
Fire, from the frying pan into the—305
Fire, sacred or divine; divine inspiration—445
Fire: there is no smoke without fire—705
Fires, between two; under two assaults—378
Firmness: with gentleness but firmness—905
First among his equals—780
First edition, a copy of a—361
First edition, as of a book—361
First, from what comes; from cause to effect—34
First sight, at—778
First things first—675
First weigh, then dare—384
Fish: you are teaching a fish how to swim—762
Fisticuffs, from words to—44
Fitting, that which is—194
Flame, from the smoke into the—305
Fleeting years glide by, alas the—362
Flies, eagle does not catch—135
Flow from the mouth; lalorrhea—464
Flowers of a bygone time—101
Follow, it does not; it is not necessarily so—712
Fondness for talking—901
Food: person who loves good food and sensuous pleasures—202
Fool is known by his remarks—404
Fools learn only by experience—400
Fools' paradise; limbo of fools—604
Foot: standing on one foot; in a precarious position—894
Footpaths of wisdom—861

For a good deed a good return—3
For any occasion that may arise—783
For each year; per year—753
For honor; for an honorary purpose—73
For honor's sake; in order to honor—513
For life eternal; forever—88
For many years! To a long life!—84
For studies and honorable achievements—900
For the purpose of appealing or captivating—66
For the thing that has arisen—783
For this; for this case only—72
For this reason; consequently; therefore—382
For those who come late, nothing but the bones—865
For two; for two only; private—16
For what good? Of what use is it?—35
For what purpose?—287
For whose good or benefit?—287
Force: by worth not by force—984
Force . . . See also under **Strength.**—981, 218, 69
Foresight is the mother of knowledge—993
Forever; always; to eternity—534
Forever and ever; for ages and ages—556
Forever; for life eternal—88
Forever: now and forever—738
Forewarned is forearmed—774, 946
Forgery, crime of—280
Forget, I am unable to—742
Forgive: to understand is to forgive—933
Former state or condition—898
Forthwith; at once; here and now—505
Fortune, every person is the maker of his own—426
Fortune . . . See also under **Good fortune, Money, Riches, Wealth,** etc.—438, 904, 71, 621
Fortunes of men, so go the—875
Forward: he who does not move forward (i.e., does not progress) falls behind—805
Forward: he who looks forward is wise—851
Forward; onward; march on—368
Fountain; from a pure fountain flows pure water—18
Fountains: draw water from unpolluted fountains—566
Francis I, words of;—after Pavian defeat—935
Frankness: to be frank; in all honesty—376

Frankness, with; with candor; with sincerity—14
Free choice; free will—602
Free hand; full authority—223
Freedom from care; freedom from worry—849
Freedom to do as one pleases; blank card—223
French Legion of Honor, motto of—512
French military award for bravery—282
Frenzy for writing; outburst of writing—473
Friend, as or like a—367
Friend, dear; cherished friend—240
Friend, faithless but unsuspected—116
Friend of the court—111
From a fresh beginning; anew—53
From a pure fountain flows pure water—18
From absurdity;—used with reference to an argument
    or reason which is regarded as inconsistent—47
From antiquity; from days of old—50
From behind; from the rear—38
From effect to cause—32
From fire comes fire—51
From head to foot; from head to heel; all over—9
From much chaff a little grain—351
From necessity; by reason of need—410
From one bad situation into another—305
From something done afterwards—413
From that day; from then on—17
From the books of—408
From the cradle; from infancy—52
From the less to the greater—27
From the nature of the thing—28
From the open heart; with the utmost sincerity—14
From the origin of the thing—54
From the particular to the general—32
From what comes later—32
From words to fisticuffs—44
Front side of a leaf, as of a book—465
Fruit: between the leaves is the fruit—569
Fruit: judge a tree by its fruit, not by its leaves—470
Frying pan into the fire, from the—305
Fundamentals need no proof—782
Futilely; without result; in pure waste—372
Future, into the; onward; march on—368

Future: my anxiety is for the future—646
Future, to live without regard to the—540

Gap much to be deplored—504
Gathering, fashionable—175
Gathering, informal—849
Gay; carefree; without worry—849
Generalization to particular case, from—34
Gentle in manner, firm in action—905
Gentleness: with gentleness but firmness—905
Gesture, beautiful; noble act—167
Gesture, empty; empty show—167
Get off one's chest—58
Get thee behind me, Satan!—958
Get thee hence, Satan!—131
Girl singer with a band—235
Give, it is noble to—830
Give not a sword to a boy—676
Give the other side a chance to be heard—154
Give the sails to destiny—303
Give to each his own—913
Give what one does not have: no one gives what he does
  not have—685
Giving: he who gives forthwith gives twice—198
Giving: it is a good thing to give—830
Glance, at first; at first glance—33
Glass, in; in the test tube—562
Glaze, pale-blue—248
Glitter: all that glitters is not gold—697
Glory comes late when it comes to one's ashes—245
Glory, done for; not for money—71
Glory: if glory comes after death, I do not hurry—874
Glory of God, all things are for the—734
Glory of yesteryear—101
Glory: so passes away the glory of the world—877
Glory: through hardships to glory—752
Glove: with a velvet glove but an iron hand—905
Glowing language—139
Glutton for books—503

Go ahead: not to go ahead is to go backward—709
God: all things are for the glory of God—734
God be merciful unto us—324
God be with you—325
God, by the gift or grace of—406
God, by the grace of—317
God: him whom God wishes to destroy he first makes
mad—798
God, house of; a hospital—516
God: If God be with us, who shall be against us!—870
God: in God we lay our hope—539
God, in the name of; for God's sake—538, 550
God: judgment of God; divine judgment—318, 582
God: thanks to God; thank the Lord—321, 484
God: we praise thee, God—919
God willing; with God's help—320
Gods, entrust the rest to the—759
Gods: fear was the first creator of gods in the world—
779
Gods: he whom the gods esteem dies growing up—799
God's help, with; God willing—320
God's right; custom demanding sexual abstinence on the
wedding night—343
Gods, twilight of the—483
God's . . . See also under **Divine.**—445, 582,
Gold in its mouth: morning hour has gold in its mouth
—659
Gold: not all that glitters is gold—697
Gold: poison is often drunk out of gold cups—962
Golden mean; happy medium—157
Good-by for now; to see you again;—*French*—150
Good-by! Take good care!—184
Good-by; till we see each other again;—*Spanish*—499
Good-by; until tomorrow—*Spanish*—500
Good day; good morning—200
Good die young—799
Good evening;—a salutation—201
Good fortune has many friends—438
Good fortune: if only they appreciated their good fortune
—904
Good heavens! My God!—654
Good living: person dedicated to a life of sensuous pleas-
ure—203

Guilt: plea of a defendant that without admitting guilt
he will make no defense—699
Guilty: he who spares the guilty punishes the innocent
—806
Guilty: he who spares the guilty threatens the innocent
—647
Guilty, not; not blameable—704
Guilty person is always timid—863

H

Habit: doing something once does not constitute a habit
—951
Hair: even a hair has its shadow—396
Hairdresser, women's—255
Hands, into thy; in your care—547
Hands-off policy of the government with regard to labor-
industry relations—594, 595
Hands, with unwashed; without preparation—525
Happiness: in happier times or years—637
Happy: hope you who are wretched, beware you who are
happy—890
Happy is he who owes nothing—439
Harbor: after so many shipwrecks, finally the harbor—
767
Harbor . . . See also under **Port**—672
Hard to please; fastidious; exacting—421
Hard work, this is really—507
Hardship: through hardships to glory—752
Hares: dead lion is insulted even by the timid hares—
663
Harmony, in; in balance; in equilibrium—533
Harmony, in; in sympathetic relationship—373
Harmony: victory is always there where harmony is—
520
Hastily; seizing the occasion—26
Hatred among physicians; medical hatred—731
Hatred among theologians—732
Hatred, let there be no—57
Hatred: without hatred; without animosity—881
Haughty, subdue the—311

Have a shipwreck in port—672
Have; desire; care—679
Have the body; bring the person before a judge—495
Hazard: at my own hazard—644
Hazardous, try something—250
He adorned everything that he touched—692
He conquers who conquers himself—978
He conquers who endures—977
He departed well—181
He gives twice who gives forthwith—198
He has half finished who has begun—328
He himself has said it—571
He is well born, well dressed, and only moderately well
    learned—183
He left under favorable conditions—181
He who dares wins—999
He who distinguishes well teaches well—801
He who does not move forward falls behind—805
He who does not progress regresses—805
He who envies is an inferior person—804
He who excuses himself thereby accuses himself—809
He who feels the benefit should also feel the burden—
    808
He who is silent thereby consents—810
He who laughs last laughs best—838
He who looks forward is wise—851
He who loses trust can lose nothing more—456
He who questions well teaches well—802
He who spares the guilty punishes the innocent—806
He who spares the guilty threatens the innocent—647
He who speaks evil hears even worse—812
He who teaches also learns—803
He who writes a thing down will remember it as well as
    if he had read it twice—807
He who writes reads twice—807
He whom the gods esteem dies growing up—799
Head: big head, little sense—492
Head cook—238
Head: cool head in trying circumstances—642
Head to heel, from; from head to foot; all over—9
Healing: physician cares for the patient, nature makes
    him well—635

Health, to your;—a wish expressed on the occasion of sneezing—480

Healthy body: sound mind in a healthy body—643

Hear the other side before passing judgment—153

Heart, from the open; with the utmost sincerity—14

Heart of a lion—251

Heartbreak; sorrow; grief—278

Heartily; with warmth—160

Heaven: may you return to heaven late—866

Heaven: much on this earth, little in heaven—665

Heaven, my strenght comes from—218

Heavens: let justice be done though the heavens tumble—449

Hebrew calendar, in the—125

Hebrew religion: boy who has reached his thirteenth year and has thus become responsible for the observance of the religious law—164

Help given promptly is twice appreciated—198

Hence; consequently; therefore; for this reason—382

Hercules, wrest the club from—250

Herd: unworthy herd; common people without a name—880

Here and now; forthwith; at once—505

Heretic in matters of grammar—498

Hiatus much to be deplored—504

High distinction; blue ribbon—268

High rank calls for magnanimity—698

High society, air of—171

High with the hand; highhanded—503

Higher; still higher; ever upward—418

Highest, in the; on high—543

Highest law, greatest injustice—910

Highhanded; overbearing; arrogant—502

Him whom God wishes to destroy he first makes mad—798

Hirelings, bunch of; band of mercenaries—491

Holiday; day of festivity—457

Home; one's own home seems the most beautiful and comfortable—12

Homeopathy, doctrine of—879

Honesty, in all; in truth; to be frank—376

Honesty, with; with sincerity; with frankness—14

Honor above all—691

Honor: all is lost but honor—935
Honor and country;—a motto—512
Honor, for; for an honorary purpose—73
Honor: for the sake of honoring—513
Honor, for the sake of; in order to honor—225
Honor, from infamy to—416
Honor: let him who deserved it get the honor—744
Honor: neither to seek honor nor to spurn it—681
Honor: nothing must be placed before honor—691
Honor, with great; with great distinction—617
Honor, with; with praise—293
Honorable reparation or amends—110
Honoring, for the purpose of—225
Hood does not make the monk—286
Hope: all hope is not gone—717
Hope: I hope for better things—891
Hope: in God we lay our hope—539
Hope is not weakened, and yet—147
Hope: let each person be his own hope—892
Hope: while there is life there is hope—349
Hope you who are wretched, beware you who are happy
    —890
Horrible monster; frightful ogre—656
Horseback, on; with a leg on either side; astride—13
Hospital, esp. the main hospital of a town—516
Hospital, private; house of health—625
Hotel of God; a hospital—516
Hour flies; time flies—471
Hour: morning hour has gold in its mouth—659
Hours pass and are reckoned against us—757
House: in the house of—243, 532
House of God; a hospital—516
House of health; private hospital—625
How the manners change with the times!—729
How, when, who, what, where, etc.—815
Human faults: as long as there are men there will be
    human faults or vices—987
Humbug; pointless story; a song—233
Humor, delicate and bright; sprightly cleverness—385
Hurry slowly; make haste slowly;—*Latin*—443
Hurt: things that hurt often teach—792
Hypochondria; disease without disease—592

I am not the kind I was; I am not what I used to be—
    714
I am not the man I used to be—714
I am still learning—115
I am unable to forget—742
I do not understand—702
I do not wish to contest—699
I fear that it is so—576
I fear the man of one book—927
I fear the man who is versed in one subject—927
I fear the specialist; I fear the man who is versed in one
    subject—927
I give up to my superior—626
I have found it!—399
I have freed my soul—601
I have not, I desire not, I care not—679
I have unburdened by mind—59
I hear but I remain silent—155
I hope for better things—891
I press forward against opposition—696
I see and approve the better things but I follow the
    worse—973
I shall not die wholly; not all of me shall die—708
I think, therefore I am—252
I will conquer or I will die—975
I will observe the faith—867
Iconoclast in matters of grammar—498
Idle kings; do-nothing rulers—840
Idleness gives vices—740
If all were thus!—728
If glory comes after death, I do not hurry—874
If God be with us, who shall be against us!—870
If it is not true, it is well contrived—857
If it is permitted to compare small things with great—
    873
If it is possible it is done, if it is impossible it shall be
    done—869
If only they knew their own blessings—904
If only they were aware of their blessings—206

If things were so! Oh, if all were thus!—728
If you start, you must finish—158
If you were here, you would feel otherwise—871
If youth knew, if old age were able!—872
Ignorance of the law excuses no one—524
Ill will, kinship kindles—253
Ill will, let there be no—57
Ill will, let there be no, in the words—58
Ill will: without ill will; without malice—881
Illegitimate child; son of nobody known—458
Imitators, a servile pack!—526
Immortality: thus does one attain immortality—876
Immortality: elixir of life—365
Important; from the less important to the more important—27
Impossible, attempt to do the—775
Impossible: if it is possible it is done, if it is impossible it shall be done—869
Impossible, try the—250
Impressed by nothing, to be—693
Impression, illusory . . . See also under **Feeling.**—322, 307
Improvement: it is easier to improve than to invent—428
In a roundabout way; with evasion—751
In accordance with what is fair and good—403
In agreement; to the same effect—74
In all; all together; counting all—375
In all honesty; in truth; to be frank—376
In bad odor; in ill repute; in bad taste—370
In better years; in happier times—637
In chapel style; without instrumental accompaniment—10
In doubt; uncertain; not determined—542
In doubtful situations—541
In eternal memory—641
In express words; in explicit terms—424
In glass; in the test tube—562
In God we hope—539
In good faith—205
In high voice; aloud—21
In ill repute; in bad odor—370

In intention and in fact—119
In memory of; to the memory of (the person named)—
548
In order to honor—225
In part payment; on account—15
In passing; in an offhand manner—371
In plain language; without circumlocution—847
In proportion to the value—87
In testimony; in witness—559
In the air; on the wing—26
In the absence (of the person involved)—530
In the end; finally—22
In the first place cited—611
In the Greek fashion—23
In the heat of action, while—347
In the Hebrew year—125
In the highest degree of excellence—745
In the highest (degree); on high—543
In the home of—243
In the house of—532
In the living body;—as opposed to an experimental en-
vironment—563
In the meantime—77
In the midst of life we are in death—633
In the name of God; for God's sake—550
In the name of the Lord—551
In the name of (the person specified)—549
In the natural state—149
In the place cited above—612
In the place cited; in the passage quoted—610
In the same place (previously mentioned)—521
In the same state as before—558
In the tried manner; in the approved manner—658
In the work quoted—736
In the year before Christ—122
In the year of Christ—123
In the year of the Lord—124
In the year of the world—126
In this; in this respect; as to this matter—545
Inactivity, bored by—377
Inactivity: when I am inactive, I deteriorate—821
Incapacitated; unfit; disabled—49

Intention and fact, in—119
Intention: as much in deed as in intention—916
Intention backed by action, with—118
Intention is to be reckoned for the deed—992
Intention: with a good or noble intention—4
Interpreters, puzzle for—284
Interval of time much to be deplored—504
Intimate manner, in an; privately—16
Into thy hands; in your care—547
Intolerance: let us crush the sordid thing—359
Intricate problem worthy of any expert—327
Intuitive knowledge; intuitive understanding—855
Invention: it is easy to add to that which has already
    been invented—428
Invention: necessity is the mother of invention;—*Latin*
    —628
Invitation: request for an answer to an invitation—828
Iron hand: with a velvet glove but an iron hand—905
Irrational: him whom God wishes to destroy he first
    makes irrational—798
Irrational: those whom Jupiter wishes to destroy he
    first makes mad or irrational—819
Irremediable wound; incurable trauma—527
Irrevocable decision—501
Isn't it so?—688
Isn't it true? Isn't it so?—689
Isn't that so?—688
Issues, in undecided—541
It cannot be helped, because of the circumstances—230
It does not follow—712
It is a good thing to give—830
It is accepted—229
It is advisable to quiet turbulent waters—664
It is agreed—229
It is done; it is accomplished—431
It is finished; it is done—262
It is getting late; the hour flies—471
It is human to err—517
It is magnificent—231
It is so, I fear that—576
It is so true—918
It is the end; it is all over—460

It is understood—229
It is war; it cannot be helped—230
It suffices; it will do—908
It will do; it is enough; it suffices—908
It would be good if they appreciated their blessings—206
It would be obvious even to a blind man—961
Itself, by; in itself; as such; inherently—756
Ivory tower; place suitable for withdrawal—930

J

Jealousy, let there be no—57
Jew converted to Christianity—645
Job without a fault—915
Joy of living—578
Judaism, apostate from—645
Judge a tree by its fruit, not by its leaves—470
Judge of elegance—136
Judge of good taste; judge of elegance—136
Judge of morals—137
Judgment comes with the years—940
Judgment, mellowed good—649
Judgment of God—318
Judgment of God; divine judgment—582
Judgment, to; to common sense—78
Jumping-off point; starting point—789
Jupiter: those whom Jupiter wishes to destroy he first
   makes mad or angry—819
Just cause; righteous cause—590
Just in time; at the opportune time—31
Just so; just right—31
Justice, by; by equity; in fairness—304
Justice, by the debt of—313
Justice: let justice be done though the earth crashes—
   450
Justice: let justice be done though the heavens tumble
   —449
Justice, with; with good right; well deserved—5

𝕶

Keep your shirt on—94
Kindness, by mere;—rather than by obligation—409
Kindness; sweetness; fragrance—340
King: after the example of the king—826
King: as is the king so are the people—795
King is dead, long live the king!—597
Kings having no governing powers, allusion to—840
Kinship kindles ill will—253
Kneeling posture, in a—19
Knees, on one's; humbly—19
Knights of the Order of the Holy Ghost, blue ribbon once
    worn by—268
Know thyself; know yourself first—718
Know thyself; take stock of yourself—481
Knowledge: foresight is the mother of knowledge—993
Knowledge: intuitive knowledge; intuitive understanding
    —855
Knowledge: read all if you wish to know all—598

𝕷

Labor-industry relations, hands-off policy of the govern-
    ment with regard to—594, 595
Labor: this is really work, this is labor—507
Labors, behold the end of our—462
Labors that are accomplished are pleasant—580
Lalorrhea; a flow from the mouth—464
Lamb of God—97
Language, glowing—139
Language of truth is simple—969
Last: cobbler stick to your last—854
Last man, to the—86
Late comers: for those who come late, nothing but the
    bones—865
Laugh: he who laughs last laughs best—838
Law, body of; collection of laws—270
Law dealing with private rights; civil law—586
Law, experienced in the—584

Law governing the religious affairs of a Christian church
—585
Law: highest law, greatest injustice—910
Law of nature; a natural law—588
Law school—356
Law: where the law is uncertain, there is no law—943
Law, written; laws created by legislation—589
Laws are silent in the midst of arms (i.e., in wartime)
—878
Laws assist the vigilant—974
Laws created by legislation or enactment—589
Laws of nature are unalterable—583
Leader: as is the leader so are the followers—795
Learn: all learn from one—55
Learn: by teaching we also learn—330
Learned with book knowledge—331
Learned woman; bluestocking—441
Learned world; world of science—655
Learning: good man always learns—209
Learning: he who teaches also learns—803
Learning, I am still—115
Learning, man of much—511
Learning, realm of; domain of literature—366
Least of evils—648
Leather trousers worn by cowboys—236
Leave no stone unturned—733
Leave the rest to fate—759
Leave well enough alone—91
Leaves: between the leaves is the fruit—569
Leaves: judge a tree by its fruit, not by its leaves—470
Leaving: he left under favorable conditions—181
Left-hand page of a book, on the—466
Left-handed; clumsy; awkward—475
Leftovers: for those who come late, nothing but leftovers
—865
Leg on either side, with a; astride; on horseback—13
Legacy, unpleasant; harmful inheritance—299
Leisure breeds depravity—740
Length, at; in detail—82
Length, at; in extended form—544
Less to greater—27
Let down one's hair now and then—323

Let each person be his own hope—892
Let fate decide; give the sails to destiny—303
Let him carry away the palm who has deserved it—744
Let it be printed; a license for printing—528
Let it pass for what it is worth—960
Let justice be done though the earth crashes—450
Let justice be done though the heavens tumble—449
Let no one venture out of his province—854
Let people do as they please—594, 595
Let the experiment be made on a worthless body—448
Let the punishment be commensurate with the crime—290
Let the superior answer (for his subordinate)—834
Let there be light!—451
Let there be no excess—677
Let there be no ill will—57
Let there be no ill will in the words—58
Let things take their own course—303
Let us be judged by our deeds—888
Let us crush the sordid thing—359
Let us return to our sheep—835
Let us return to the subject (from which we digressed)—835
Let us speak good words—326
Let us turn to better things—83
Letter for letter; literally; to the letter—607
Letter, to the; literally—81
Letter, to the; precisely;—*French*—24
Letter: written letter lasts—608
Letter: written letter remains—995
Letters, beautiful; fine literature—178
Letters, empire of—366
Letters: written letters remain—609
Level head in a difficult situation—642
Library: from the library of—408
License of poets—603
Licentiousness; disorderly life—166
Life: as is the life so is the end—797
Life, disorderly; licentiousness—166
Life, ephemeral nature of—633, 757
Life eternal, for—88
Life is short; time flies—923

Living organism, in the;—as opposed to an experimental environment—563
Living: we live more by example than by reason—420
Logic of coming to a conclusion—822
Long words; words a foot and a half long—868
Longing, intense; ardent desire—322
Look at the possible outcome—833
Look for the woman in the case—241
Look forward: he who looks forward is wise—851
Look to the end; consider the outcome—459
Look to the end; consider the possible outcome—833
Lord be praised! Thank God!—482
Lord, direct us; Lord, show us the way—335
Lord, in the name of the—551
Lord, in the year of the—124
Lord: the Lord be with you—337
Lord: the Lord is my enlightenment—336
Lord . . . See also under **God.**—734, 324, 325, 406, 317, 798, 516, 870, 539, 538, 550, 318, 582, 321, 484, 919, 320
Lord's Supper, the—226
Loss, as a complete; without result whatever—372
Loss, feeling of painful—322
Lost soul; person morally debased—109
Love and wisdom: to love and to be wise at the same time is scarcely granted even to a god—105
Love is blind; love and wisdom do not mix—105
Love note; love letter—196, 197
Love of money—112
Love of one's country guides—345
Love or money, for neither—680
Love: with love; with tenderness—257
Low neckline in a woman's dress—316
Luck, agreeable change of—579
Luck: good luck follows bad luck—766
Luck: with good luck; with a kindly fate—188

𝕸

Mad: him whom God wishes to destroy he first makes mad—798
Mad: those whom Jupiter wishes to destroy he first

makes mad or angry—819

Made after some event but having retroactive effect—413

Madness, agreeable form of—104

Magnificent; excellent; splendid;—*French*—623

Magnificent; excellent; splendid;—*Spanish*—622

Magnificent, it is—231

Main dish of a meal—761

Make a monumental mistake; err by the whole extent of the heaven—929

Male dancer, esp. professional—301

Malice: without malice; without ill will—881

Man; mankind; species that is man—479

Man of courage—251

Man of honor; man of his word—474

Man of letters; author of literary works—509

Man of much education or learning—511

Man of one book, I fear the—927

Man of responsibility, in Hebrew religion—164

Man of the pen; author; writer—510

Man who appreciates literature—509

Man who knows one book or subject, I fear the—927

Man who lives by writing; author—510

Man . . . See also under **Person.**—173, 202, 203, 426, 136, 108, 892, 109, 268, 107, 111, 425, 944

Maneuver; blow; stroke—273

Mankind; species that is man; man—479

Manliness: with all of one's manliness—928

Manner: agreeable in manner, firm in deed—905

Manner, in the approved or tried—658

Manner of doing reveals the man—899

Manner . . . See also under modifying term, as **Mysterious.**—751

Manners, against good—263

Manners change with the times—729

Manners, lacking in; crude; left-handed—475

Manners: Oh the times, oh the manners!—729

Man's job: do not give a man's job to a boy—676

Many blows fell even an oak—668

Many learn from one—55

Marine Corps, motto of—862

Mass, in a; in a body; in a group—369

Men who live by the pen; writers; authors—478
Mendacious: splendidly mendacious; admirably deceptive —893
Mental depression; disease without disease—592
Mental disease, functional; disease without disease—592
Mental strength: physical and mental strength—839
Mentally qualified to handle one's affairs, not—703
Mercenaries, band of; bunch of hirelings—491
Mercy: God be merciful to us—324
Mercy, stroke of—274
Merit: for merit; for due worth—772
Merit, to those who—182
Method of disproving a proposition by showing its absurdity when amplified—825
Method of disproving a proposition by showing its absurdity when carried to conclusion—825
Method of proving a proposition by showing that its opposite is foolish—825
Methods, against accepted—263
Methods: radical methods result in radical reactions—51
Midday, after; after noon—764
Middle class of society—211
Middle-of-the-road course is best—144
Middle of the road, happy—157
Might: with all of one's might—928
Military action, French award for bravery in—282
Mind and body, with both—118
Mind, brilliant; wit—173
Mind, creative; creative reason—721
Mind: from a clean mind come clean thoughts—18
Mind: I have unburdened by mind—59, 601
Mind, not in one's right—100
Mind: not of sound mind—703
Mind, of sound; sane—256
Mind: small matters occupy light minds—746
Mind: sound mind in a healthy body—643
Mind: speech is the index of the mind—864
Mind: vigor of body and mind—839
Mind: well-balanced mind in arduous circumstances— 642
Mind, with calmness of—95
Mindful and faithful—638

Motto: higher; ever upward—418
Mouth, with open; in the manner of a young bird; hungrily; avidly—7
Move every stone; make every effort—733
Move, sudden and successful—273
Much: from much chaff a little grain—351
Much in few words—667
Much on this earth, little in heaven—665
Murder, body of the victim in a case of—269
Muscular stiffness following death—837
Music; at the tempo chosen by the performer—11
Music, practice piece in—398
Musical composition, esp. one played for its artistic value—398
Musical composition, whimsical—222
My anxiety is for the future—646
My dear; my sweetheart—613
My faith! Upon my faith!—614
My God! Good Heavens!—654
My strength comes from heaven—218
Mysterious manner, in a; in a secret way—751
Mystery of mysteries—138
Myth agreed upon for convenience to explain something bothersome—427

Nail: you hit the nail on the head—64
Naked; in the natural state—149
Name assumed by an author; pen name—701
Name: common people without a name; nameless multitude—880
Name: in the name of (the person specified)—549
Name: shadow of a great name remains—896
Name, under this; by this title—508
Name worth remembering; remarkable name—639
Name . . . See also under qualifying term, as **Assumed, Pen, Theater,** etc.—701, 700
Nameless multitude; common people without a name—880
Narration: by badly narrating a story is spoiled—627
Natural law; law of nature—588

Nature, debt to; one's life—314
Nature does not jump; nature makes no sudden changes —671
Nature: laws of nature are unalterable—583
Nature of the thing or situation, from the—28
Nature: physician cares for the patient, nature makes him well—635
Nature strives for perfection—670
Nausea: even to nausea; to the point of disgust—954
Nausea, to the point of—85
Necessary proposition—784
Necessity, case of—224
Necessity, from; by reason of need—410
Necessity is the mother of invention; —*Latin*—628
Neckline, low, in a woman's dress—316
Need, by reason of; from necessity—410
Negotiation: by negotiation, not by arms—453
Neither by entreaty nor by bribe—680
Neither by prayer nor by bribe—680
Neither to seek honor nor to spurn it—681
Nest: to each bird its own nest is beautiful—12
Never give up; never despair—695
Never: now or never; now or not at all—727
New broom sweeps clean—949
New disputes on old accounts—45
News: no news is good news—725
Nicety, to a; just so—31
Night, a good; a night of pleasure—207
Night: better counsel comes after a night's sleep—189
Nightcap; drink taken before retiring—208
No day without a line; no day shall pass without the addition of a line to one's writing—724
No news is good news—725
No one dissenting; unanimously—683
No one gives what he does not have—685
No one is born without vices—988
No one is wise enough all by himself—687
No one suffers punishment for his thoughts—684
No rule is without an exception—726
Nobility obliges; rank involves responsibility—698
Nobility: virtue is the only true nobility—885
Noble act; beautiful gesture—167

One must yield to the demands of the changing times—
921
One out of many—352
One subject: I fear the man who is versed in one subject
—927
One time: doing something one time does not constitute
a habit—951
One witness is regarded as no witness—925
One wrong does not excuse another wrong—564
One . . . See also under **Person.**—173, 202, 203, 426, 136,
108, 892, 109, 268, 107, 111, 425, 944
Oneself: not for oneself but for all—713
Onward; forward; march on—368
Opinion: from the consensus of opinion of all people—
350
Opinions: as many men, so many opinions—820
Opposition: I press forward against opposition—696
Orally; by word of mouth—46
Oration: brevity is the essence of a good oration—591
Ordeal, arduous—163
Ordeal, trial by—318
Order, irrevocable; decision that cannot be revoked—
501
Order requiring the authorities to bring a specified
prisoner into court—495
Organism, in the living;—as opposed to an experimental
environment—563
Origin: from the origin of the thing—54
Origin, of the same—363
Original: precisely as recorded in the original; word for
word, letter for letter, and point for point—964
Orthodox; right-thinking; well-disposed—193
Others, with many—294
Ourselves: between ourselves; between us; confidential-
ly;—*French*—379
Ourselves: not for ourselves alone—707
Out of action; disabled—49
Out of the depths, as of feeling—307
Out of the mouth of babes comes the truth—412
Outcasts; wretched; unfortunate ones—599
Outcome, be mindful of the; consider the end—459
Outcome, consider the; perceive the end—161
Outcome, look to the possible; look to the end—833

Outcome, regardless of; without discrimination—41
Outcry of reproach to a betraying friend—394
Outlet, as for emotions; exit—315
Outline; rough sketch, as of a plot—353
Outlook, fair; fine view—177
Outside the main dish; an appetizer—515
Outside the work; something extra—514
Overbearing; arrogant; highhanded—502
Overthrow, sudden, as of an established government—275
Oxford University, motto of—336

ℙ

Pacts are to be kept—743
Page, left-hand, of a book—466
Page, right-hand, of a book—465
Painful subject: mention a painful subject; touch a wound—917
Pale-blue glaze, as of porcelain—248
Palm: let him carry away the palm who has deserved it —744
Pamphlets have their own fate—496
Pants down, with the; unprepared—525
Paper, license to print or publish a—528
Pardon: to understand all is to pardon all—933
Partiality: without partiality; without bias; without prejudice—882
Particular to the general, from the—32
Party to whom the rights of another have been transferred—162
Passage quoted, in the—610
Passing glory: so passes away the glory of the world—877
Passion, crime of; crime impelled by unrequited love—279
Passions, for the purpose of appealing to—66
Past, glory of the—101
Path: beaten path is the safe path—970
Patience: be patient with others, and others will be patient with you—442

Patience brings all things in time—937
Patience surpasses science—748
Patient: after the death of the patient, the doctor—134
Patient: physician cares for the patient, nature makes
　him well—635
Patriotism serves as a guide—345
Pause is the greatest remedy for anger—631
Pay, without; not for money; for glory—71
Payment, in part; on account; to the credit of an ac-
　count—15
Peace be with you; peace to you—749, 750
Peace: may he (or she) rest in peace—829
Peace: may his bones rest in peace—653
Peculiarity, delightful—104
Peers, before one's—267
Peers, spokesman for a group of—780
Pen, a battle with the; epistolary war—494
Pen name; name assumed by an author—701
People: as is the king so are the people—795
People rule, the—827
People: so many people, so many opinions—820
People: What will people say?—800
People . . . See also under **Persons.**—478, 477
Perfection, nature strives for—670
Performer, at pleasure of; at the tempo chosen by the
　performer;—esp. in music—11
Perhaps it will be pleasant some day to reminisce even
　about these things—467
Permission: with the permission of the superiors—296
Permission, with your; at your pleasure—187
Permission, with your kind—291
Permit, esp. for the publication of a book—528
Perpetual memory of the thing, in—554
Perpetuity, in; for eternity—553
Perseverance and virtue, by—261
Perseverance brings results—747
Perseverance, with; with diligence—259
Person, clever; beautiful spirit—173
Person devoted to good food and sensuous pleasures—
　202
Person devoted to good living—203
Person, every, is the maker of his own fortune—426
Person fastidious in his tastes—136

Person having base tendencies—108
Person, intellectual; beautiful spirit—173
Person is master of his own fate—426
Person: let each person be his own hope—892
Person morally debased—109
Person of high distinction—268
Person slavishly obedient to another—107
Person who advises a court in some special field—111
Person who dedicates himself to the sensuous pleasures of life—203
Person who is disliked during his lifetime is often loved after his death—425
Person who loves good living—202
Person who tries to be everywhere at the same time—944
Person . . . See also under **Man, Woman, One,** and under modifier, as **Curious, Intermediary, Quick-tempered,** etc. 479, 251, 474, 509, 511, 927, 164, 510, 241, 339, 441, 440
Personal; private; in an intimate manner—16
Persons of the pen; authors; writers—478
Persons of the same flour; birds of a feather—477
Persons . . . See also under **People.**—795, 827, 820, 800
Pertaining only to this; for this case only—72
Philistine; crude; lacking in social graces; left-handed—475
Physical and mental strength—839
Physician cares for the patient, nature makes him well—635
Physician, heal thyself; put your own house in order first—634
Physicians, disgrace of—737
Physicians, hatred among—731
Physicians, puzzle for—285
Pilate, words used by, in presenting Christ—354
Pinnacle: through adversity to the pinnacle—754
Pivot: thing is on a pivot—832
Place cited, in the—610
Place cited, in the above—612
Place cited, in the first—611
Place, in the above-mentioned—612
Place, in the original;—whether normal or abnormal—557

Place suitable for withdrawing from reality, as for contemplation—930
Plaintiveness, with;—as in music—333
Plan: without plan and without justification—848
Play of words; pun—577
Player, at the tempo or with the expression chosen by the—11
Plea of a defendant that without admitting guilt he will not make a defense—699
Pleasanter subjects, let us turn to—83
Pleasing confusion or disorder—166
Pleasing insanity—104
Pleasure, at one's; as much, or as often, as one wishes—80
Pleasure, at your; with your permission—187
Pleasure: everyone enjoys his own form of pleasure—903
Pleasures of life, keen enjoyment of the—578
Pleasures: person who is dedicated to the sensuous pleasures of life—203
Pleasures: person who loves the sensuous pleasures of life—202
Plenty; enough and more than enough—853
Poem; poetry; epic—233
Poetic license; artist's right to deviate—603
Point-blank; to one's face; so close as to burn the doublet—8
Point: jumping-off point; starting point—789
Point of comparison—788
Point, salient; conspicuous feature—789
Point, to the; just right—31
Point: word for word, letter for letter, and point for point—964
Point . . . See also under the qualifying term, as **Turning.**—832
Pointless story; humbug; a song—233
Poison: do not take the antidote before the poison—675
Poison is often drunk out of gold cups—962
Policy, change of—319
Policy of action; new line of action—319
Policy of letting business owners set their own rules of competition—594, 595
Policy of noninterference—594, 595

Political move, sudden and forceful—275
Polysyllabic words; words a foot and a half long—868
Port, have a shipwreck in—672
Port . . . See also under **Harbor.**—767
Position, by virtue of one's—411
Position, in the normal;—as where found—557
Position of delicate reserve; ivory tower attitude—930
Possibility, in a state of; potentially—555
Possible: if it is possible it is done, if it is impossible it
    shall be done—869
Post-mortem inquest—565
Potentially; in a state of possibility—555
Power, with all of one's—928
Powers, with united—260
Practice makes perfect; practice makes the craftsman—
    945
Practice makes the expert—463
Practice makes the master—945
Practice piece in music; an exercise—398
Practices, according to good—860
Praise, endless desire for—596
Praise: they are silent—they praise enough—914
Praise, with, as for scholastic work—293
Praise, with great; with great honor—617
Praise, with the greatest—630
Praise, with the highest—909
Prank; whim; caprice—222
Prayer: neither by prayer nor by bribe—680
Precarious position, in a; standing on one foot—894
Precautionary measure, as a—67
Pre-eminently; in the highest degree of excellence—745
Prefatory remark for a statement which may sound dis-
    paraging—58
Prejudice: without prejudice; without bias; without
    partiality—882
Prejudices, for the purpose of appealing to—66
Preparation, without; with unwashed hands—525
Prepared in all things—552
Prerequisite, vital; essential quality—883
Prescription instruction directing patient to take the
    medicine when the need arises—783
Present, to live for the—540

Quotation: in the first place quoted—611
Quotation: in the passage or place quoted—610
Quotation: in the place cited above—612

ℜ

Race, of the same—363
Radical methods result in radical reactions—51
Rage for speaking; frenzy for talking—472
Random, at; without discrimination—41
Rank, admitting to the same—68
Rank involves responsibility; nobility obliges—698
Rat on one's friends; desert one's party; turn one's coat
    —931
Rather to die than to be defiled—768
Rationale for deciding—822
Read all if you wish to know all—598
Ready for all eventualities—552
Reality: something that blinds a person to reality—769
Really! Indeed!—614
Reap: you sow for yourself, you reap for yourself—926
Rear, from the; from behind—38
Reason, creative; creative mind—721
Reason for deciding—822
Reason: without rhyme and reason—848
Recapitulation, in; in summary—374
Recollections, from the earliest; from the cradle—52
Reduction to absurdity—825
Reference books used by authors—132
Refuge from anxieties—886
Regarded apart from any particular case; in the abstract
    —531
Regress: he who does not progress regresses—805
Regress: not to progress is to regress—709
Relationship, sympathetic, in a state of—373
Reliance upon oneself: each person must rely upon him-
    self—892
Religion: as far as one's religion permits—953
Remain faithful to the old order—895
Remark, undiplomatic; tactless observation—437
Remarkable name; name worth remembering—639

Sacred fire; divine inspiration—445
Sacrifice, at considerable—20
Sacrifice: to the final sacrifice; to the altars—953
Safe way: well-trodden way is the safe way—970
Safeguard, as a—67
Safety: there is safety where there are many counselors
   —845
Said: all has been said; all has been covered—934
Sail where the winds blow—303
Salient point; conspicuous feature—789
Salt, with a grain of—292
Same as (that mentioned before)—523
Same effect, to the—74
Same, the; the same as that mentioned previously—522
Sanatorium, private; house of health—625
Sanction; permit;—esp. for the publication of a book—
   528
Sanctuary, right of—342
Sand without lime—140
Sane; of sound mind—256
Satan: Get thee behind me, Satan!—958
Satan: Get thee hence Satan!—131
Say: you say it well—176
Saying much with few words, practice of—667
Scamp a duty—842
Scar: and even when a wound is healed the scar remains
   —397
Scholars: betrayal of the scholars—939
Scholars, with notes by many—295
School for the teaching of fine arts—358
School of medicine—357
Science, world of—655
Sciences, circle of the—739
Scientific knowledge, sum of—739
Sculpture, roughhewn form of a—353
Seasoned discretion; mature wisdom—649
Secret: everybody's secret; an open secret—858
Secret: nothing burdens so heavily as a secret—836
Secret, ultimate—138
Secret way, in a; in a mysterious manner—751

Shifts, in; taking alternate turns—102
Ship, do not give up the—673
Ship: do not put all your goods in one ship—952
Shipwreck in port, to have a—672
Shooting so close as to burn the doublet—8
Shortcomings: everyone has his own shortcomings—902
Shot which ends the suffering of an executed person—
    274
Sick man, dreams of a—92
Sick man, vain dreams of a—93
Sides: change sides; desert one's party; turn one's coat—
    931
Sighing much; groaning much—666
Sight, at first; from the beginning—33
Silence, deep or profound—103
Silence: he who remains silent about an issue is regarded
    as consenting—810
Silence of virulent critics, allusion to—914
Silence: their silence is eloquent—348
Silence: their silence is praise enough—914
Silent: they are silent—they praise enough—914
Simple; unadorned; in the natural state—149
Sincere and fair; righteous and loyal—344
Sincerity, with; in good faith—205
Sincerity, with utmost; from the open heart—14
Sinew of proof; the "nerve" of the proof—687
Singer, female—235
Singer, female professional—221
Singer, female, with a band—235
Singing in chapel style, without instrumental accompani-
    ment—10
Singing marked by skillful vocal display—172
Singing marked by virtuosity and purity of tone—172
Site, in the normal;—as where found—557
Situation as it existed before—898
Situation: as the situation demands—414
Situation calls for other aid and different defenders—715
Situation, difficult, worthy of any expert—327
Situations, in doubtful; in uncertain matters—541
Situations: unusual situations call for unusual measures
    —159

Skeletons, dance of the—300
Skepticism, with a certain amount of—292
Slander, there is art even in—387
Sleep, twilight; partial sleep—297
Small matters occupy light minds—746
Small things: if it is permitted to compare small things
   with great—873
Smoke into the flame, from the—305
Smoke: there is no smoke without fire—705
Snake in the grass—116
Sneezing, wish for health expressed upon—480
Snows of yesteryear—682
So go the fates of men—875
So many people, so many opinions—820
So passes away the glory of the world—877
So true is it; it is so true—918
Social convention is a tyrant—955
Social graces, lacking in; crude; left-handed—475
Social position imposes obligations—698
Society, admission to a—195
Society, air of high—171
Society, fashionable; high society—168
Soft and smooth; sweet;—said esp. of music—332
Soldier's first experience of enemy fire—163
Solution of one difficulty by introducing another—694
Some remedies are graver than the perils they are sup-
   posed to avert—490
Someday it will be pleasant to remember these things—
   497
Something absolutely necessary—883
Something bitter or unpleasant—106
Something of me shall survive—708
Something that blinds a person to reality—769
Something that diverts attention from the facts—769
Son: as is the father so is the son—794
Son of nobody known; bastard—458
Song; ballad—233
Song, beautiful—172
Song, short; little song; ditty—234
Sorrow for something unattained—322
Sorrow, great; heartbreak; overwhelming grief—278
Sorrowful mood, in a; with plaintiveness—333

Stable; secure; settled—192
Stand upon the old ways—895
Standing on one foot; in a precarious position—894
Stars: through adversities to the stars—755
Stars: through difficulties to the stars—754
Stars: thus does one go to the stars—876
Start: do not start unless you mean to finish—678
Start, from a new; from a fresh beginning—53
Starting point; jumping-off point—789
State: in the state in which the thing or situation is or
    was at the time spoken of—558
State in which (the affair is or was)—897
State of affairs as it existed before—898
State, stroke of; sudden political move—275
Steadfastness in the midst of difficulties—980
Step by step one goes quite far—747
Steps: you will waste your steps there—994
Stiffness of body after death—837
Stiffness of death—837
Stimulus: serve as a stimulus for others—770
Stock, of the same—363
Stone: leave no stone unturned—733
Stone, move every; make every effort—733
Stories, unlikely; old wives' tales—117
Story: by badly narrating, a story is spoiled—627
Story fits you; story is told of you—310
Straits: through straits to noble ends—752
Strength: courage arouses strength—981
Strength: my strength comes from heaven—218
Strength, to the extreme of one's—69
Strictest law, severest injury—910
Stroke; maneuver; blow—273 ·
Stroke of mercy—274
Stroke of state; sudden political move—275
Stroke, revolutionary; stroke of state—275
Stroke which brings something unpleasant to an end—
    274
Strong through faith—407
Student: designating the transfer of a student which
    admits him to the same rank or degree—68
Studies and honorable achievements, for—900
Study in music; practice piece—398
Style of a ballad, rendered in the—1
Style proves the man—899

ℭ

That without which something is impossible—883
The more gently one commands, the better he is complied with—650
Their silence is praise enough—914
Thelogocial hatred; hatred among theologians—732
Theory, based on;—rather than on experience—34
There is art even in speaking evil—387
There is no law where the law is uncertain—943
There is no need for reasoning regarding principles—782
There is no relying on appearance—469
There is no smoke without fire—705
There is safety where there are many counselors—845
There is still hope—147
There will be another day—717
Thing is on a pivot, i.e., at a turning point—832
They abound with charming faults—61
They are silent—they praise enough—914
They condemn that which they do not understand—298
They pass and are reckoned;—an allusion to time—757
Thing is on a pivot, i.e., at a turning point—832
Things become clear in time; time reveals everything—924
Things change (with the years)—735
Things done; facts; deeds—831
Things of the past; snows of yesteryear—682
Things that hurt often teach—792
Things that should be noted—720
Things that should be observed and remembered—720
Things that were once vices are now customs—791
Things which accompany or form the environment of a legal case—831
Things worth noting—719
Things worth observing and remembering—719
Things worthy of remembrance—640
Think before you leap—384
Thinking, without; hastily—26
This, as to; in this; in this respect—545
This is really work, this is labor—507
This is the difficult part of the job—507
This line has attracted nothing—506
Those whom Jupiter wishes to destroy he first makes mad or angry—819

Thought and act, with both—118
Thoughts: no one suffers punishment for his thoughts
—684
Throng, indescribable; common people without a name—
880
Through adversities to the stars—756
Through adversity to the pinnacle—754
Through difficulties to splendor—752
Through difficulties to the highest achievements—755
Through difficulties to the stars—754
Through hardships to glory—752
Through narrow ways to noble ends—752
Thus does one go to the stars—876
Thy will be done!—452
Till we meet again; till we see each other again—
German—156
Till we meet again; to see you again;—*French*—150
Time and space, in the endlessness of—546
Time changes all things—735
Time clarifies things; things become clear in time—924
Time: days pass and are reckoned against us—757
Time explains everything; everything becomes clear in
time—924
Time flies; life is short—923
Time flies; the hour flies—471
Time has wings; time flies—923
Time immemorial, from; from eternity—48
Time: interval of time much to be deplored—504
Time is the devourer of things—922
Time is the greatest changer of things—632
Time, just in; at the opportune time—31
Time, on the passing of—362
Time passes swiftly; time flies—923
Time reveals everything—924
Time: spirit of the time—1000
Time: truth is the daughter of time—593
Time: truth will out in time; truth is the daughter of
time—968
Time: you will waste your time—994
Times change and we change with them—920
Times, in happier; in better years—637
Times: manners change with the times—729

Too late to do good—133
Too late to do good; after the death of the patient—134
Tool of another's will; minion—107
Tormenting attractiveness—169
Touch a wound; touch a tender spot—917
Touch: he adorned everything that he touched—692
Traitors: translators are traitors—938
Transgression, light; minor fault—289
Transgression: one transgression follows another—443
Translators are deceivers; translators are traitors—938
Translators, puzzle for—284
Trauma, incurable; irremediable wound—527
Treatment, and he grows worse with—91
Treatment is worse than the disease—91
Treatment: some treatments are worse than the diseases
    they are supposed to cure—490
Tree: judge a tree by its fruit, not by its leaves—470
Trend of the time—1000
Trial by ordeal—318
Tribunal . . . See also under Court. 111, 907, 906
Tribute used in diplomas: with great honor or praise—
    618
Tribute used in diplomas: with praise or honor—293
Trifle at the proper time—323
Trifles: great man does not occupy himself with trifles
    —135
Trifling matters occupy small minds—746
Triumph: he triumphs who perseveres—977
Trouble: do not anticipate trouble—675
Trousers, leather, worn by cowboys—236
True: I fear that it is true—576
True: if it is not true, it is well contrived—857
True: it is so true; so true is it—918
True to life; in the natural state—149
Trust, but watch whom you trust—454
Trust: he who loses trust can lose nothing more—456
Truth conquers all things—976
Truth fears nothing except concealment—966
Truth: great is the truth, and it prevails—619
Truth: great is the truth, and it will prevail—618
Truth, in; in all honesty; to be frank—376
Truth is the daughter of time; truth will out in time—
    593, 968

Truth: language of truth is simple—969
Truth: out of the mouth of babes comes the truth—412
Truth overcomes all obstacles; truth conquers all things
    —976
Truth: seek the truth—793
Truth speaks in simple terms—969
Truth: suppression of truth—911
Truth: suppression of truth is the suggestion of a false-
    hood—912
Truth: What is truth?—811
Truth will out in time—593
Truth will out in time; truth is the daughter of time—
    968
Truth will prevail—967
Truth will triumph in the end—967
Try something hazardous or the impossible—250
Try: this try ended in failure—506
Turbulent waters, it is advisable to quiet—664
Turkish decree; irrevocable order—501
Turmoil, serene amid—843
Turn one's coat; desert one's party—931
Turning point: thing is at a turning point—832
Twilight of the gods—483
Twilight sleep; partial sleep—297
Two, for; for two only; private—16
Twofold application or use, having—114
Tyrant: custom is a tyrant—955

U

Ubiquitous person; person who seems to be everywhere
    at the same time—944
Ultimate secret—138
Ultracrepidarianism, allusion to—854
Unanimously; no one dissenting—683
Unanimously; to the last one—86
Unattained, sorrow for something remaining—322
Unborn; in the womb—561
Unburden: I have unburdened my mind—59, 601
Uncertain; in doubt; not determined—542
Uncertain matters, in—541

Unclean hands, with; without preparation—525
Uncontrollable urge to find fault—213
Uncontrollable urge to make speeches—214
Uncontrollable urge to write—215
Undependable in one thing, undependable in everything
—434
Understand so that you may believe—567
Understand, they condemn that which they do not—298
Understand: to understand is to forgive—933
Understanding: intuitive understanding; intuitive knowledge—855
Understanding: to understand all is to pardon all—933
Understood, it is—229
Unfit; incapacitated; disabled—49
Unfortunate ones, the; the outcasts; the wretched—599
Unit, as a; all together—560
United powers, with—260
United States, motto of—352
United States of America—395
Unity: in unity there is strength—520
Universal proposition—785
Universal reward: ingratitude is the universal reward
—950
Universally held opinion, from the—350
Universe, spirit of the—117
University: designating a transfer which admits the
student to the same rank or degree—68
Unknown author—151
Unpleasant, something; something bitter—106
Unprepared; with unwashed hands—525
Until it shall be corrected—338
Until tomorrow; good-by—500
Until we see each other again; good-by;—*Spanish*—499
Unusual situations call for unusual measures—159
Unwilling: benefit cannot be bestowed on one who is not
willing—186
Unworthy herd; common people without a name—880
Unwritten law; common law—600
Upon my word! Upon my faith!—614
Us: not for us only—707
Usage is a cruel taskmaster—955
Usage of words, accepted—786

Use, having a twofold—114
Use not abuse: to use, not to abuse—957
Use, of what; for what good?—35
Use, proper; misuse does not militate against proper use
   —62
Uterus, in the; unborn—561

𝖁

Vaguely; indefinitely; obscurely—535
Vain dreams of a sick man—93
Vain, in; as a complete loss—372
Valor: discretion is the better part of valor—993
Value, according to the; in proportion to the value—87
Vanity; excessive self-esteem—113
Vanquish the haughty—311
Velvet glove: with a velvet glove but an iron hand—905
Venture: this venture has yielded nothing—506
Verily; in truth; in fact—376
Very best; cream of the cream—277
Vices and customs: things that were once vices are now
   customs—791
Vices: as long there are men there will be vices—987
Vices: everyone has his own vices—902
Vices, idleness breeds—740
Vices: no one is born without vices—988
Victory is always there where concord is—520
Victory or death: I will conquer or I will die—975
View, fine; fair outlook—177
Vigilant: laws assist the vigilant—974
Vigor of body and of mind—839
Vigorous old age—283
Virtue alone ennobles a man—983
Virtue conquers all—334
Virtue in trouble—537
Virtue is praised, and usually starves—982
Virtue is the only true nobility—885
Virtue overcomes all temptations—334
Virtue, rewards of—773
Virtue: secure through virtue—985
Virtue, with constancy and—261

Vitality: demonstrate vitality or spirit—771
Vivacity; spirit; lively wit—385
Voice, and beyond this nothing—996
Voice, in loud; in loud tones—21
Voice, with a living; orally—46

W

Wailing; crying; puling—959
Waiting: everything comes properly to him who knows
   how to wait—937
Walls of a city or college, within the—570
War between the gods and their enemies, in Germanic
   mythology—483
War, it is—230
War name; name under which one battles—700
War of all against all—179
War of the pen; a battle with the written word—494
War, such are the hazards of—230
War unto death; fight to the bitter end—493
Warmth, with; heartily—160
Warning, on the value of a—946
Wars, horrible wars!—174
Wartime: laws are silent in wartime—878
Waste, in pure; as a complete loss—372
Waste: you will waste your steps there—994
Wasting time, you are—536
Watchmen: Who shall watch the watchmen themselves!
   —814
Water under the bridge; snows of yesteryear—682
Waters, turbulent, it is advisable to quiet—664
Way: Lord show us the way—335
Way, the wrong; against the grain—36
Way: well-trodden way is the safe way—970
Way . . . See also under qualifying term, as **Secret.**—751
We are bound to death; we are mortal—312
We are but dust and shadow—787
We live more by example than by reason—420
We praise thee, God—919
We shall see; we shall find out—722
We shall see what we shall see—723

Where are you going? Where are you headed for?—817
Where the law is uncertain, there is no law—943
Where the wind their course guides—790
Where there is a right, there is a remedy—942
Which see; which look up—818
While the iron is hot—347
While the work is hot—347
While there is life, there is hope—349
While they are silent, they cry out—348
Whim; caprice; prank—222
Whimpering; whining; puling—959
Whimsical musical composition—222
Whining . . . See under **Whimpering.**—959
Whither goest thou?—817
Whither the Fates beckon—816
Who does not know the rest!—232
Who is able? Who knows?—813
Who is the man who never his bread with tears ate!—
 998
Who knows? Who is able?—813
Who shall watch the watchmen themselves!—814
Who, what, where, by what means, why, how, when?—
 815
Whoever begins something must also finish it—997
Whoever says A must also say B—997
Whole, as a; in a mass—369
Whole, considered as a; all together—560
Whole, on the; in recapitulation—374
Whole world is wise after something has happened, i.e.,
 after the event—936
Why, how, when, who, where, etc.—815
Will, free; free choice—602
Will . . . See also under **Wish.**—322
Willing man: fates guide the willing man, the unwilling
 they drag along—346
Win: he who dares wins—999
Win: he wins who bears patiently—977
Wind: where the wind their course guides—790
Wing, on the; in the air—26
Wisdom comes with the years—940
Wisdom: enough of eloquence but too little of wisdom
 —852

Wisdom: footpaths of wisdom—861
Wisdom, mature; seasoned discretion—649
Wisdom: no one is wise enough all by himself—686
Wisdom: prudence is the mother of wisdom—993
Wise: dare to be wise—152
Wise: dare to be wise; dare to be sensible—850
Wise: he who looks forward is wise—851
Wise man learns from the fault of another—417
Wise: word to the wise is sufficient—965
Wish, ardent; passionate desire—322
Wit, brevity is the soul of—591
Wit, display one's—771
Wit, lively; spirit; vivacity—385
With a favoring god; with good luck—188
With a good intention—4
With a grain of salt—292
With a leg on either side; astride; on horseback—13
With a living voice; by word of mouth—46
With all of one's might—928
With all of one's power—928
With; among; in the service of—243
With both mind and body—118
With candor; with sincerity; from the open heart—14
With courage and faith—120
With diligence; with perseverance—259
With equanimity—95, 96
With gentleness but firmness—905
With God's help; God willing—320
With good right; with justice; well deserved—5
With great praise; with great honor—617
With love; with tenderness—257
With many others—294
With notes of various scholars—295
With open mouth, as a young and hungry bird—7
With praise, as for scholastic work—293
With sincerity; in good faith—205
With spirit; with animation—160
With spirit; with zest—258
With the greatest praise—630
With the highest praise—909
With the permission of the superiors—296
With unwashed hands; without preparation—525

With your kind indulgence—291

Withdrawal: place suitable for withdrawing from reality, as for contemplation—930

Within the walls (as of a city or a college)—570

Without affectation in style—847

Without bias; without partiality; without prejudice—882

Without care; without worry; without anxiety—849

Without discrimination; with open mouth, in the manner of a hungry young bird—7

Without fear and without reproach—846

Without hatred; without animosity—881

Without ill will; without animosity—881

Without instrumental accompaniment; in chapel style—10

Without plan and without justification—848

Without prejudice; without bias; without partiality—882

Without previous thought or preparation—415

Without rhyme and reason—848

Without which not; without which nothing; vital pre-requisite—883

Witness: in witness; in testimony—559

Witness: one witness is no witness—925

Witness: writ commanding a person to appear in court and testify as a witness—906

Woman as the cause of all evil—241

Woman is changeable; woman is fickle—339

Woman, learned; literary woman; bluestocking—441

Woman: look for the woman in the case—241

Woman of letters; literary woman; a learned woman—440

Woman . . . See also under **Person.**—173, 202, 203, 426, 136, 108, 892, 109, 268, 107, 111, 425, 944

Womb, in the; unborn—561

Wonder at nothing; admire nothing—693

Wool over the eyes—769

Word: and once uttered, a word flies irrevocably away—392

Word for word, letter for letter, and point for point—964

Word of mouth, by; orally—46

Written words last—609
Wrong and awry; at cross purposes—41
Wrong and right, both; rightly or wrongly—40
Wrong: one wrong does not justify another wrong—564
Wrong way, the; against the grain—36
Wrong way, the; wrong; wrongly—39

𝔜

Year: for each year; by the year; yearly—753
Year regarded as approximate, word designating—246
Yearly; annually; per year—753
Yearnings, set a limit to your—228
Years: alas, the fleeting years glide by—362
Years bring wisdom; years bring judgment—940
Years, from the early or tender—37
Years, in better; in happier times—637
Years teach more than books—575
Yes indeed; certainly—573
Yesteryear, glory of—101
Yesteryear, snows of—682
Yore, of; from antiquity—50
You are teaching a fish how to swim—762
You are writing in water—536
You hit the nail on the head—64
You may break me, but you shall not bend me—468
You must accept me as I am—991
You say it well—176
You sow for yourself, you reap for yourself—926
You tell it splendidly—176
You touched the matter with a needle; you hit the nail
    on the head—64
You will waste your steps there—994
You will waste your time—994
Young bird, like a, with open mouth; avidly—7
Young: he whom the gods esteem dies young—799
Youth, bloom of—169
Youth: If youth knew, if old age were able!—872
Youthful old age—283

Z